PICTO
CATALOGUE AND HANDBOOK OF PICTORIAL POSTCARDS AND THEIR POSTMARKS 1980

M. R. Hewlett B.A.
Ron Mead Joan Venman
B. H. Swallow

First Published by B.P.H. Publications Ltd. in 1971
1st Edition - August 1971
2nd Edition - September 1971
3rd Edition - April 1973
4th Edition - November 1976
2nd Issue - March 1976
5th Edition - November 1977
6th Edition - January 1979
7th Edition - November 1979

B.P.H. Publications Ltd.,
Citadel Works, Bath Road.
Chippenham, Wilts., SN15 2AA
Tel. Chippenham 50391/2

ISBN 0 902633 65 1

PRINTED IN GREAT BRITAIN BY PICTON PRINT,
CITADEL WORKS, BATH ROAD, CHIPPENHAM, WILTS, ENGLAND SN15 2AA

TABLE OF CONTENTS

PREFACE - THE ADDRESS SIDE

The Philatelic side of Postcard collecting i.e. postmarks, stamps and 'first days', has seen, during 1979, the steady annual average rise in prices to allow for the inflation rate which seems like 20% according to the price levels attained.

As I have said, in earlier years, philately is a long established hobby such that prices have stabilised, subject to inflation of course, so that, except for 'plums', price rises have not been meteoric as for some of the 'picture' postcards.

There has been an upsurge in interest in the numeral cancellations especially for the ordinary duplex and the sideways duplex postmarks.

Postmark collecting can still be a reasonably cheap form of hobby so that the demand for postcards carrying good strikes (and I emphasise GOOD) has strengthened in 1979 so that my advice to you is to buy now while comparatively low prices persist.

Owing to the shortage of good, genuine lots at auction (and the shortage of good, genuine albums coming into dealers' shops for sale) the competition for even mediocre material has raised PICTURE postcard prices higher and higher so that the buyer with a knowledge of postmark prices has just that extra edge on less well-informed collectors or dealers, to enable him to outbid those who do not value BOTH sides of the postcard! One good postmark can make all the difference to the value of a lot so study the postmarks is my advice to you for 1979/80.

Box, Wiltshire
October, 1979

M. R. Hewlett, B.A.

Frontally-applied Chinese Cachet – Emperor's Funeral – Price £6.

PREFACE

Now that the postcard hobby has reached full adulthood in the collecting world I am delighted to welcome R.F.Postcards (Joan Venman and Ron Mead) on to the Editorial Board of Picton's Catalogue because, quite frankly, pricing the Picture Side has become too much of a task for one person. How Maurice copes with the Postmark side on his own surprises me but no doubt his now being a Senior Citizen gives him more time! This year the help from Joan and Ron has been particularly helpful because of my move from London Road to the Great Western Antique Centre in Bath.

This last year has seen the fine topographical card really establish itself as the premier category as regards numbers of collectors even if still at relatively low prices compared with the ever-popular advertising cards and certain 'artists'. All in all there has been a general rise in prices following not only inflation but the increasing number of collectors coming into the hobby. The future for postcards looks very healthy indeed.

B. H. Swallow

Bath
October, 1979

RF POSTCARDS PREFACE

Although we have been trading in Postcards since 1972, having come in with the "new wave" of collecting, this is the first time we have ventured "into print", and we are gratified that Messrs Hewlett & Swallow should think us qualified to join them.

We have re-organised the Catalogue for the picture side into sections which we feel will be more helpful to both collectors and dealers, especially as we have cross-referenced wherever necessary.

Our pricing is based upon the latest retail prices with special emphasis on photographic cards which have grown enormously in popularity during 1979 and look all set to continue that growth.

We realise, of course, that there is still a lot of work to be done, but we hope to continue, as we have started, our part, in making Picton's a truly comprehensive postcard catalogue.

Essex, 1979

Joan Venman & Ron Mead

NOTES ON THE PRICES SHOWN IN THIS CATALOGUE

Where in the pricing, a high and a low figure are quoted, the reader must use his own judgement and decide where the specimen under consideration lies. There is no *rigid price control* on postcards. It is in the eye of the beholder and maybe London and some of the larger conurbations are accustomed to higher prices than those ruling in the more rural areas and isolated towns. The reader must grade such cards for himself, but this catalogue does indicate whether a card is common, medium valued or a rarity, according to the prices shown.

Condition
Is very important.
Prices in the catalogue are for subject cards in perfect and topographical cards in acceptable condition.
If a mint (unused) card has a defect then the price can be halved at once and if the defect is really serious the card can become valueless. With used (usually stamped and cancelled) cards if the writing or postal markings are unsightly even further reductions in price have to be made. Remember that a glossy transparent 'bag' covers a multitude of sins so take the card out before buying!

Many postcards are illustrated by an artist whose name appears somewhere on the card. In many cases it will be found that the 'value of the artist' exceeds that of the value of the classification. Users of the catalogue should therefore check the artist section before finally pricing a card. To a lesser degree certain manufacturers/publishers/printers are so popular that the price for that aspect often exceeds that of the theme price so that a quick consideration of 'maker' is also necessary before finally pricing a card.

Auction Sales
There are some devoted solely to Postcards but other Auctions of Stamps, Books and even Local House Contents carry a few lots of postcards in most sales. It is becoming an increasing source of supply but most cards change hands nowadays at the many postcard fairs, antique fairs, etc.

Procedure for Pricing
An *Unused Card*, i.e. with no writing or adhesive stamp upon it at all, is much easier to price than a used one with an adhesive stamp. With unused cards if there is no artist or publisher to consider then just look for the appropriate classification in the index. If the card is *used*, then having decided its value had it been *UNUSED*, one has another aspect to consider. Is the postmark of greater value than the classification?

Some people actually read the writing on their used cards and at times the information thereon over-rides all the previous valuation possibilities (it is then Ephemera – yet another factor!) Sometimes the signature is a valuable autograph.

To settle a vexed question about pricing one cannot add up all the valuations arising from the above facets of pricing. Normally the highest factor of pricing should be taken with maybe a little 'rounding up' if other valuable factors co-exist.

Although this catalogue mainly covers the British Isles, for convenience, certain 'foreign and Commonwealth' classifications are noted if they are of frequent appearance on the British Scene.

CARDS PRODUCED AFTER 1939

Obviously they lack 'age' but how long will it take for picture postcards of all classifications of such 'later vintages' to acquire a premium over their normal shop sale price for use in correspondence? Here is where the younger collectors can use their perspicacity to seek out those 'modern' cards which are going to appreciate in the long term – they will – BUT WHICH WILL BE THE PRICE LEADERS?

GLOSSARY

APPLIQUE

Postcards to which some 'material' has been attached are termed 'applique'. It may take the form of cloth to adorn part of the picture or a small piece of metal like a medal, or even human hair.

COMPOSITES

Where a number of postcards are required in order to make up a large picture, the set of such cards is referred to as a composite set. They were usually issued in sets of between three to twelve cards.

EMBOSSED

These have part of the surface of the card pressed upwards and are found for example on heraldic subjects and many greetings cards.

ETHNIC

These refer to postcards depicting the indigenous race(s) of any country in their characteristic costumes and/or activities.

FABS

These are cards which have upon them silk, a square with a printed design which could be removed and used for patchwork decoration. The cards are adverts for Sharpe's of Bradford.

GRUSS AUS

This is German for 'Greetings from' and to some extent was the originating idea for pictorial postcards, i.e. folks away from home sent such cards to their friends and relations to indicate where they were staying. This is a very popular Continental classification.

c) Scene changes or **metamorphorics**. These are the rarest of the H.T.L.'s. On holding them to the light a *different* scene appears.
The instruction 'Hold to Light' is often printed in an oblong box on the picture side in:-

French - Carte Transparente
German - Bitte Gegen Das Licht Zu Halten
English - Pray hold this card up to the light
and you shall see a charming sight

'MAGIC CARDS'

These reveal a picture when heat or friction or a chemical is applied to them.

MONTAGE

These are postcards depicting persons or scenes composed of postage stamps etc., cut up and pasted upon the card to produce the picture involved. Chinese stamps seem the most commonly used and then Japanese. Much time must have been spent in producing them.

PANEL CARDS

These are postcards produced on very thick card.

PATRIOTICS

These usually carry the flag or emblem of the country concerned with some national event or characteristic indicated. Highly popular cards, usually coloured and often embossed.

PULL OUTS

Where strips of views, etc. are folded under flaps on the face of the cards and 'pulled out' to view.

REWARD CARDS

The London County Council Education Department used to issue postcards to pupils who excelled in various aspects of scholastic life. Other Education Authorities have issued them, as well as other types of organisations.

TINSEL (or GLITTER)

Many cards bear this minor embellishment, i.e. best described as a minor metallic application which glistens. It is the most common form of adornment.

UNDIVIDED BACKS

When postcards using adhesive stamps were first allowed in 1894, the back, in postcard collectors' parlance, was reserved exclusively for the address and the adhesive stamp, i.e. no message was permitted on the back. The message if any

HOLD TO LIGHT

(H.T.L. ABBREVIATION)

These are all cards which you *'look through'* against some form of light. There are three types:-

a) **'Cut outs'**. The construction of the card is such that coloured (yellow or blue are very popular) translucent material is introduced to cover the 'cut out sections' so that on holding to light, the cut out sections, being transparent, allow the light through, hence their name - transparencies. The cards are usually thicker than normal. They often depict 'windows' at night with 'light' shining therefrom.

b) Colour changes or **chameleons**. On holding to the light, the the *colours of the* **same** *picture*, as the name suggests, change, usually for the better, because the normal appearance of the card is drab.

had to be on the picture side so the picture did not fill the whole of the front, but consisted of a vignette and space for the message. Undivided backs persisted until late in 1902, although Regulations permitted the divided back to be used in 1897.

VIGNETTE

A small picture on the front of a postcard, usually found on cards with undivided backs. A message could be written on the space left.

WRITE AWAY

A pictorial card bearing the opening phrase of a sentence which required completion by the sender. Very popular in Edwardian Days as holiday correspondents seemed 'at a loss for words' and this type of card made life easy for them.

ARTISTS

The artists listed in this section will also be found cross-referenced under subject headings where appropriate. General artists are listed here only.

Artist	Subject	Price
A.E.	Comic	60☐
Abeille Jack	Glamour	£16☐
Acker Flori von	General	40☐
Ackroyd W.M.	Animals	£1.50☐
Adams M.	General	40☐
Adams Will	Comic	£1.50☐
Addison W.G.	General	40☐
Ainsley Anne	Animals	50☐
Albertini	Glamour	£2☐
Aldin Cecil	Advert	-
	Animals	£2☐
Allan A.	General	40☐
Allen S.J.	General	40☐
Alys M.	Children	£1☐
Anders O.	Animals	£2☐
	Comic	£2☐
Anderson V.C.	Children	£1☐
Armitage A.	General	50☐
Asti Angelo	Glamour	£1.50☐
Attwell, Mabel Lucie	Children	
Early		£1.50☐
Middle		£1☐
Later		75☐
Austerlitz E.	Comic	£2☐
Austin E.H.S.Barnes-	Animals	£3☐
Aveling S.	General	£1.50☐
Azzoni A.	Children	£1☐
Bairnsfather Bruce	Comic/Military	£1☐
Baker H. Granville	Military	£3☐
Ball Wilfred	General	40☐
Bamber George A.	Comic	75☐
Barber C.W.	Children	75☐
	Glamour	£1.50☐
Barham S.	Children	£2☐
Barnes A.E.	Animals	£1.50☐
Barnes G.L.	Comic	£1☐
Barribal, L.	Children	£2☐
	Glamour	£3☐
	Theatre	£6☐
Barraud A.	General	30☐
Bask W.	General	30☐
Basch Arpad	Art Nouveau	£80☐
Bates Marjorie C.	General	40☐
Bebb Rosa	Animals	£1☐
Becker C.	Military	£5☐
Bee	Comic	30☐
Beer Andrew	General	60☐
Belcher George	Comic	£4☐
Bell Hilda	General	30☐
Bender Paul	General	20☐
Bennett Godwin	General	20☐
Beraud, N.	Military	£3☐
Berkeley Edith	General	40☐
Berthon, Paul	Art Nouveau	£75☐
Bertiglia A.	Children	£2.50☐
Bianchi	Glamour	£3☐
Biggar J.L.	Comic	50☐
Billings M.	General	75☐
Birch Nora Annie	Children	30☐
Birger	Art Deco	£6☐
Blair Andrew	General	40☐
Bob	Comic	£1☐
	General	50☐
Boileau Philip	Glamour	£3☐
Bolton F.N.	General	30☐
Bompard S.	Glamour	£4☐
Borrow W.H.	General	50☐
Bothams W.	General	40☐
Bottaro E.	Glamour	£3.50☐
Bottomley George	Glamour	£1.50☐
Boulanger Maurice	Animals	£3☐
	Comic	£2☐
Bourillon	Military	£2☐
Boutet Henri	Art Nouveau	£18☐
Bowers S.	General	30☐
Bowley M.	Children	£1☐
Boyne T.	General	30☐
Bradshaw, Percy V. (PVB)		
	Comic	£5☐
	Political	£5☐
Braun W.	Glamour	£5☐
Breanski Arthur de	General	60☐
Brett Molly	Children	£1☐
Bridgeman Arthur W.	General	50☐
Brisley Nora	Children	50☐
Broadrick Jack	Comic	75☐
Browne Tom	Comic	£2-£3☐
	PosterAdverts	£25-£50☐
	Weekly Telegraph	£4☐
	Captain Mag	£4☐
	Cathedrals etc	£2.50☐
Brundage Frances	Children	£4☐
	General	£2.50☐
Brunelleschi, U.	A. Deco	£80☐
Buchanan Fred	Comic	£1.50☐
Buchell, A.	Theatre	£5☐
Bull Rene	Comic	£2.50☐
Burger R.	General	40☐
Burton F.W.	General	50☐
Bushby Thomas	General	40☐

Artist	Category	Price
Busi Adolfo	A. Deco	£4□
Butcher Arthur	Children	75□
	Glamour	£1.50□
Buxton Dudley	Comic	75□
Caldecott Randolph	Children	60□
Carey John	Comic	75□
Carline George	General	50□
Carrere F.O.	Glamour	£6□
Carruthers W.	General	50□
Carter Reg.	Comic	75□
Carter Sydney	Comic	75□
	General	£1.50□
Cassiers H.	General	£4□
Cattley P.R.	Comic	50□
Chalker	Comic	50□
Chandler E.	Comic	75□
Charlet J.A.	Glamour	£5□
Chiostri	Art Deco	£16□
Christiansen Hans	Art Nouveau	£80□
Christie, G.R.	Comic	
	Pre-1918	£1.50□
	After 1918	£1□
Christy F. Earl	Glamour	£2□
Clapsaddle Ellen H.	Children	£2□
	General	£2□
Clarkson R.	General	30□
Cloke Rene	Children	£1□
Coates A.	General	30□
Cobbe B.	Animals	£1.25□
Colborne Lawrence	Comic	£1.25□
Cole Edwin	General	30□
Coleman W.S.	Children	£1.50□
Colombo, E.	Glamour	£3□
	Children	£1.50□
Combaz, Gisbert	Art Nouveau	£70□
Comicus	Comic	75□
Cooper A. Heaton	General	50□
Copping Harold	Glamour	£2□
Corbella T.	Glamour	£4□
Cordingley G.R.	General	40□
Corke C. Essenhigh	General	50□
Cowham Hilda	Children	£1.50□
	Comic	£1.50□
Crackerjack	Comic	£1.50□
Cramer, Rie	A. Deco	£12□
Croft Anne	General	20□
Crombie C.M.	Comic	£1–£2.50□
Croxford W.E.	General	30□
Cubley H. Hadfield	General	50□
Cynicus	Comic	
	Court Sized	£6+□
	Early U/B	£1.75□
	Last train, etc.	£1.50□

Artist	Category	Price
	Later	£1□
Daniell Eva	Art Nouveau	£55□
Dauber	Comic	£1.50□
Davey George	Comic	£1.50□
Daws F.T.	Animals	£1□
Dexter Marjorie M.	Children	50□
Diefenbach K.W.	Glamour	£8□
Diemer Michael Zeno	General	£6□
Dinah	Children	30□
Dirks Gus	Comic	75□
Dobson H.J.	General	40□
Donadini jr.	Animals	£1.50□
Douglas J.	General	30□
Driscoll	Comic	30□
Drummond Norah	Animals	£1□
Ducane E. & F.	General	40□
Dudley Tom	General	40□
Dudley	Comic	30□
DuFresne Paul	Glamour	£3□
Duncan Hamish	Comic	75□
Duncan, J. Ellen	Children	75□
Dupuis Emile	Military	£4□
Dwiggins C.V. (Dwig.)	Comic	£3□
Dyer W.H.	General	50□
Dymond R.J.	General	30□
Earnshaw H.C.	Comic	60□
Ebner Pauli	Children	£4□
Edwards Edwin	General	40□
Ellam	Comic	£1□
Emanuel Frank L.	General	40□
Endacott S.	General	£1□
Esmond (Germs)	Comic	£4□
F.S.	Comic	75□
F.W.	Comic	75□
Fabiano F.	Glamour	£5□
Feiertag K.	Children	£2□
Fidler Alice Luella	Glamour	£2□
Fidler Elsie Catherine	Glamour	£2□
Finnemore J.	General	60□
Fisher Harrison	Glamour	£2.50□
Fitzpatrick	Comic	25□
Fleury, H.	Comic	£1□
	Railway	£1.50□
Flower Charles E.	General	75□
Folkard, Charles	Children	£2.50□
Fontan Leo	Glamour	£6□
Forres Kit	Children	40□
Foster Gilbert	General	40□
Foster R.A.	General	30□
Fradkin, E.	Children	40□
French Annie	Art Deco	£35□
Fuller Edmund G.	Comic	£2.50□
Fulleylove Joan	General	50□

Artist	Category	Price
Furniss Harry	Political	£4☐
Gallon R.	General	50☐
Gassaway Katherine	Children	£2☐
Gay Cherry	Children	30☐
Gayac	Glamour	£5☐
Gear, M	Animals	50☐
Gerald Brian	General	30☐
Gerbault H.	Glamour	£4☐
Gibson Charles Dana	Glamour	£2.50☐
Giglio	Glamour	£3☐
Gill Arthur	Comic	£2.50☐
Gilmour	Comic	50☐
Gilson T.	Comic	75☐
Gladwin May	Comic	£1.50☐
Golay Mary	General	75☐
Goodman, Maud	Children	
	Tuck Chromo-Litho	£4☐
	Hildersheimer	50☐
Gozzard J.W.	General	50☐
Graeff	Comic	75☐
Graf Marte	A. Deco	£5☐
Grant Carleton	General	30☐
Grasset Eugene	Art Nouveau	£27☐
Green Roland	Animals	50☐
Greenaway, Kate	Children	
	1903 printing	£50☐
Greiner M.	Children	£2.50☐
Gretty G.	General	30☐
Grey Mollie	Children	30☐
Grimes	Comic	50☐
Grosze Manni	A. Deco	£5☐
Grunewald	A. Deco	£5☐
Guerzoni C.	Glamour	£5☐
Guillaume	Comic	£3☐
Gunn A.	Glamour	£3☐
Guy T.	General	30☐
Hager Nini	Art Nouveau	£25☐
Hannaford	General	30☐
Hansi	Children	£4☐
Harbour, Jennie	A. Deco	£6☐
Hardy, Dudley	Comic	£4☐
Hardy, Florence	Children	£2.50☐
Hardy, F.	A. Deco	£5☐
Hardy F.C.	Military	£1.50☐
Hassall, John	Advert	£25-£35☐
	Comic	£4☐
	Theatre	£10☐
Haviland Frank	Glamour	£3☐
Hayes F.W.	General	40☐
Hayes Sydney	Animals	60☐
Henckel Carl	Military	£4☐
Henry Thomas	Children	50☐
Herouard	Glamour	£6☐
Hey Paul	General	£4☐
Heyermans John A.	General	30☐
Hier Prof. van	General	£1.50☐
Higham Sydney	General	75☐
Hilton Alf	Comic	75☐
Hines B.	General	50☐
Hodgson W. Scott	General	20☐
Hoffmann H.	General	40☐
Hohenstein A.	Art Nouveau	£10☐
Holloway Edgar A.	Military	£2☐
Horrell Charles	Glamour	£1.50☐
Horsfall, Mary	Glamour	£1.50☐
Horwitz Helena	Glamour	£2.50☐
Howard C.T.	General	50☐
Hudson Gerald	Military	£2☐
Hughes Lloyd	Comic	50☐
Hunt Edgar	Animals	£1☐
Hunter Mildred C.	Animals	75☐
Hurst Hal	Comic	£1.50☐
Hutchinson F.	General	40☐
Hyde Graham	Comic	£2☐
Ibbetson, Ernest	Comic	£2.50☐
	Military	£3☐
Innes, John	Ethnic	£2☐
Jacobs, Helen	Children	£4☐
James Frank	Animals	50☐
James, Ivy Millicent (IMJ)	Children	£2☐
Jarach A.	Glamour	£6☐
Jenkins G.H.	General	50☐
Johnson M.	General	40☐
Josza Carl	Art Nouveau	£27☐
Jotter	General	40☐
	Hotels	£1.50☐
	Better Cards	£1.50☐
Kammerer R.	General	30☐
Karaktus	Comic	50☐
Kaskeline Fred	Glamour	£2☐
Kaufmann J. C.	Animals	£1☐
Keene Elmer	General	30☐
Keene Minnie	Animals	30☐
Keesey Walter M.	General	30☐
Kennedy A.E.	Animals	£1.50☐
Kidd, Will	Children	£1.25☐
King A. Price	General	50☐
King Jessie M.	Art Nouveau	£40☐
Kinnear J.	General	40☐
Kinsella E.P.	Advert	
	Children	£1.50-£5☐
	Comic	£1.50-£5☐
	Theatre	£6☐
Kirchner, Raphael	Art Nouveau	
Glamour	Early	£50☐
	Middle Period	£25☐

Artist	Subject	Price
Kirchner, Raphael	Bruton Galleries	£12□
Kirk A.H.	General	40□
Kirkpatrick	General	50□
Klein Christina	General	
	Chromo-Litho	£2□
	Later issues	75□
Kley, Paul	General	£5□
Koehler Mela	A. Deco	£18□
Konopa	Art Nouveau	£18□
Kosa	Art Nouveau	£65□
Kulas J.V.	Art Nouveau	£30□
Kyd	Literary	£5□
Lamb Eric	General	40□
Lambert H.G.C.Marsh-	Children	£1.50□
Larcombe, Ethel	A. Nouveau	£20□
Lasalle, Jean	Glamour	£2□
	General	50□
Lauder C.J.	General	40□
Lautrec, H.de Toulouse	A. Nouveau	£300–£500□
Lawes H.	General	40□
Leete Alfred	Comic	£1.50□
Leigh Conrad	Military	50□
LeMunyon, Pearle Fidler	Glamour	£2□
Leonnec G.	Glamour	£6□
Lessieux E. Louis	Art Nouveau	£27□
Lester Adrienne	Animals	60□
Lewin F.G.	Comic	75□
Lilien	General	£4□
Lindsell L.	General	£1□
Long L.M.	General	20□
Longstaffe Ernest	General	50□
Loreley	A. Deco	£8□
Lowe Meta	Children	75□
Ludgate	Comic	50□
Ludovici, A	Children	£3□
	Comic	£2.50□
	Political	£3□
M.S.M.	Glamour	£10□
Mac	Animals	50□
	Comic	50□
Macdonald A.K.	A. Nouveau	£15□
Mackain F.	Comic	75□
Macleod F.	Comic	75□
McGill, Donald	Comic	
	Early dated	£2.50□
	Pre-1914	£1.50□
	Later	75□
	"New"	10□
McIntyre R.F.	General	40□
McNeill J.	Military	£8□
Maggs J.C.	Coaching	75□
Maguire Bertha	General	50□
Maguire Helena	Animals	£1.50□

Artist	Subject	Price
	General	60□
Mailick A.	General	£2.50□
Mair H.Willebeek le	Children	£4.50□
Mallet Beatrice	Children	75□
Manavian V.	Comic	£1□
Marechaux C.	Glamour	£3□
Martin L.B.	Comic	40□
Martineau Alice	General	£1.50□
Martino R. de	General	50□
Mason Finch	Comic	£1.50□
Mastroianni D.	General	50□
Mataloni, G.	A. Nouveau	£10□
Mathison W.	General	30□
Maurice Reg.	Comic	75□
Mauzan A.	Children	£2□
	Glamour	£4□
May, Phil	Comic	
	Write-aways	£4□
	Oilette	£2.50□
Maybank, Thomas	Children	£1□
Mercer Joyce	A. Deco	£4□
Meredith Jack	Comic	50□
Merte O.	Animals	£1.50□
Meschini, G.	A. Deco	£8□
Metlicovitz, L.	A. Nouveau	£10□
Meunier Henri	Art Nouveau	£70□
Meunier Suzanne	Glamour	£8□
Miller Hilda T.	Children	£2.50–£4□
Milliere Maurice	Glamour	£6□
Monestier C.	Glamour	£3□
Montague R.	General	40□
Montedoro M.	A. Deco	£15□
Moore, F.	Railway	75□
Moreland Arthur	Comic	£2□
	Political	£4□
Morgan F.E.	Comic	75□
Morris M.	General	75□
Moser Koloman	Art Nouveau	£60□
Mostyn Dorothy	Glamour	£2□
Mostyn Marjorie	Glamour	£2□
Mouton G.	Glamour	£5□
Mucha Alphonse	Art Nouveau	£80□
Nailod C.S.	Glamour	£4□
Nam Jacques	Glamour	£6□
Nanni G.	Glamour	£4□
Nap	Comic	75□
Nash A.A.	Children	£1□
Newton G.E.	General	40□
Ney	Glamour	£6□
Nielsen Vivienne	Animals	£1□
Noble, Ernest	Comic	£1□
Norman Parsons	General	50□
Norwood A.Harding	General	30□

Artist	Subject	Price
Noury Gaston	A. Nouveau	£30☐
Nystrom Jenny	Glamour	£4☐
O'Beirne F.	Military	£8☐
O'Neill Rose	Children	£4☐
Opper F.	Comic	75☐
Orens Denizard	Political	£20☐
Outcault, R.F.	Children	75☐
Outhwaite Ida R.	Children	£1.50☐
Owen Will	Comic	£3☐
Palmer Sutton	General	40☐
Pannett R.	Glamour	£1.50☐
Parker N.	Animals	30☐
Parkinson Ethel	Children	£3☐
Parlett Harry	Comic	75☐
Parlett T.	Comic	50☐
Parr B.F.C.	General	20☐
Parsons, F.J.	Railway	£1☐
Pantella B.	A. Nouveau	£15☐
Paterson Vera	Children	75☐
Payne Arthur C.	General	50☐
Payne, G.M.	Glamour	£1.50☐
	Comic	£1.25☐
Payne, Harry	Military	
	Tuck Vignettes	£10☐
	Tuck "Empire"	£10-£15☐
	Badges & Wearers	£7☐
	Defenders	£5☐
	Hildersheimer	£6☐
	Stewart & Woolf	£6☐
	Oilettes	£2-£4☐
	Rural General	£2-£6☐
Pearse Susan B.	Children	£2.50☐
Pellegrini E.	General	£2☐
Peltier L.	Glamour	£5☐
Penley Edwin A.	General	40☐
Penny Theo	Comic	75☐
Penot A.	Glamour	£5☐
Pepin Maurice	Glamour	£5☐
Peras	Glamour	£5☐
Percival E.D.	General	40☐
Perly	Comic	30☐
Person Alice Fidler	Glamour	£2☐
Pfaff C.	General	£3☐
Phillimore, R.P.	General	£1.50☐
Phipson, E.A.	General	50☐
Pinder Douglas	General	20☐
Pinkawa Anton	Art Nouveau	£25☐
Piper George	Children	60☐
Pirkis	Comic	
Col.		£2.50☐
B/W		£1.50☐
Pope Dorothy T.	Animals	£3☐
Popini	A. Nouveau	£20☐

Artist	Subject	Price
Poulbot Francisque	Children	£2☐
Preston Chloe	Children	£1☐
Purser, Phyllis	Children	75☐
Pyp	Comic	£2☐
Quatremain W.W.	General	50☐
Quinnell Cecil W.	Glamour	£2☐
Quinton, A.R.	General	50☐
	Tuck Oilettes	75☐
Quinton F.E.	General	30☐
Quinton Harry	Comic	75☐
Raemaekers Louis	Political	£2☐
Rambler	General	30☐
Ramsey George S.	General	30☐
Rankin George	Animals	£1☐
Rappini	Glamour	£3☐
Rauh Ludwig	Glamour	£10☐
Reckling L.C.	General	40☐
Reichert C.	Animals	£1☐
Reiss Fritz	General	£4☐
Reynolds Frank	Comic	£3☐
Ribas	Glamour	£6☐
Richardson Agnes	Children	£1.50☐
Richardson R.E.	General	50☐
Right	Comic	75☐
Ritter Paul	General	£2.50☐
Roberts Violet M.	Comic	£2☐
	Animals	£2☐
Robida A.	General	£3☐
Robinson W. Heath	Comic	£3☐
Rodella G.	Glamour	£3☐
Rose, Freda Mabel	Children	30☐
Rossi J.C.	A. Nouveau	£30☐
Rostro	Political	£6☐
Rousse Frank	General	40☐
Rowland Ralph	Comic	£1.50☐
Rowlandson G.	General	£1☐
Rowntree Harry	Comic	£3☐
Rylander	Art Deco	£6☐
Sager, Xavier (Salt Lake)	Glamour	£6☐
Salmony G.	Glamour	£3☐
Sandford H. Dix	Comic	£1.50☐
Sauber	General	£4☐
Schonflug, Fritz	Comic	£3☐
Schubert H.	Glamour	£3☐
	General	£3☐
Schweiger L.	General	£4☐
Scottie	Glamour	£4☐
Scrivener Maude	Animals	£1☐
Severn Walter	General	50☐
Shand C.E.	Art Deco	£6☐
Shaw W. Stocker	Comic	£1☐
Shelton S.	General	30☐
Shepheard G.E.	Comic	£1.50☐

Simkin R.	Military	£8☐
Simonetti A.M.	Glamour	£3☐
Smith Jessie Wilcox	Art Deco	£12☐
Smith, Syd	Comic	50☐
Somerville Howard	Glamour	£3☐
Sonrel Elisabeth	Art Nouveau	£28☐
Sowerby Millicent	Children	£3☐
Chromo-litho	Children	£4.50☐
Spatz	Comic	£1☐
Sperlich T.	Animals	£1☐
Spurgin, Fred	Comic/Patriotic	£1.25+☐
	Glamour	£2.50☐
Stannard H.	General	40☐
Stead A.	General	20☐
Steinlen, Alexandre	A. Nouveau	£60☐
Stenberg Aina	Art Nouveau	£8☐
Sternberg V.W.	Children	75☐
Stewart J.A.	Military	£2.50☐
Stoddart R.W.	Comic	75☐
Stokes G.Vernon	Animals	50☐
Stower Willi	General	£6☐
Studdy G.E.	Comic	£1.50☐
Bonzo	Comic	£2☐
Syd	Comic	75☐
T.B.M.	Comic	50☐
Tait	Comic	40☐
Tam Jean	Glamour	£6☐
Tarrant Margaret W.	Children	75☐
Taylor, A.	Comic	30☐
	Children	35☐
Tempest, D.	Children	75☐
	Comic	75☐
Terzi A.	Glamour	£5☐
Thackeray Lance	Comic	
	Write-away	£4☐
	Oilettes	£2.50☐
Thiele, Arthur	Animals	£4☐
	Comic	£4☐
Thomas Bert.	Comic	£1.50☐
Thompson E.H.	General	40☐
Toussaint M.	Military	£4☐
Trick E.W.	General	20☐
Trow	Comic	20☐
Turrian E.D.	Art Nouveau	£22☐
Twelvetrees C.H.	Children	£1.75☐
Uden E.	General	40☐
Underwood, Clarence F.	Glamour	£2☐
Upton Florence K.	Children	£7☐
Usabal L.	Glamour	£3☐
Vallet L.	Glamour	£5☐
Valter Eugenie M.	Animals	75☐
Valter Florence E.	Animals	75☐
Vaughan E.H.	General	40☐
Voellmy F.	General	£3☐
Wain, Louis	Animals	
	Vignettes used	£8☐
	Vignettes unused	£12+☐
	Later issues	£10☐
	Tuck Oilettes	£10☐
Walker F.S.	General	40☐
Wanke, Alice	A. Deco	£10☐
	Children	£5☐
Ward Dudley	Comic	£1☐
Ward Herbert	Military	£2.50☐
Ward Vernon	General	40☐
Wardle Arthur	Animals	£1☐
Warrington E.	General	30☐
Watson C.M.West	Animals	75☐
Wealthy R.J.	Animals	£1☐
Wennerberg, B.	A.Deco	£8☐
West A.L.	Animals	75☐
West Reginald	General	30☐
White Brian	Children	30☐
White Flora	Children	£1☐
Wichera, R.R.	Children	£3☐
	Glamour	£4☐
Wiederseim G.G.	Children	£4☐
Wielandt Manuel	General	£4☐
Wilkin Bob	Comic	40☐
Williams Madge	Children	60☐
Williams Warren	General	40☐
Wimbush Henry B.	General	50☐
Wimbush Winifred	General	50☐
Wood, Lawson (Spy)	Comic	£1.50☐
	Prehistoric	£2.50☐
	Gran'pop	£2☐
Woodville R.Caton	Military	£2☐
Wright Gilbert	General	75☐
Wright Seppings	General	40☐
Wuyts A.	Children	£3☐
	Glamour	£4☐
Young A.	General	50☐
Zandrino Adelina	Glamour	£5☐
Zirka C.	Glamour	£3☐

ADVERTISING

POSTER DESIGNS

This section includes cards actually used for advertising promotion as well as those like Tucks Celebrated Posters which were well-known posters produced in miniature and published in sets or series for collectors. Prices vary and you would expect to pay more for popular series, well-known or collectable products and cards designed by prominent artists such as John Hassall, Kinsella, Cecil Aldin, Tom Browne, etc. All cards listed are COLOURED, except where otherwise indicated.

Tucks Celebrated Posters	
Common designs. e.g.	
Dewars, Cadburys, etc.	£12–£15☐
Other Designs	
(Later Series are rarer)	£25–£50☐
Answers	£2☐
Barbours Linen Thread	£16☐
Berrys Boot Polish	£20☐
Birds Custard	£25☐
British Army Posters	£25☐
Bryant & Mays	£12☐
Campbells Soups (Weidersheim)	£30☐
Camp Coffee	£25–£35☐
Continental Tyres	£30☐
C.W.S.	£10☐
Fry & Sons	£15–£35☐
Fry & Sons T. Browne designs	£12☐
Gossages Soap	£30☐
Holbrooks Ltd.	£18☐
Hornimans Tea	£15–£25☐
H.M. & Co's Famous Posters	£30☐
Keiller, James	£12☐
Nestles Milk	£25☐
North British Rubber Co.	£30☐
Raleigh Cycles	£16☐
Shell	£25☐
Shell (reprints set)	£1☐
Skipper Sardines	£8+☐
Tit-bits	£2☐
Viscan Pet Foods	£5☐
Wood Milne Rubber Heels	£15☐

Tuck's Celebrated Poster – a rarely seen example – £45.

TOBACCO

Adkins Tobacco (Tom Browne Posters)	£50☐
Grays Cigarettes (views)	60☐
R. & J. Lea (Chairmans Series)	£2☐
R. & J. Lea (Chairmans Series) suppliers' imprint	£4☐
Ogdens	£35☐
Philips, Godfrey	20☐
Sarony, Nicholas	75☐
Wills	£35☐

Aviation
Circus
Motoring
Railway
Shipping
Theatre

See under these headings

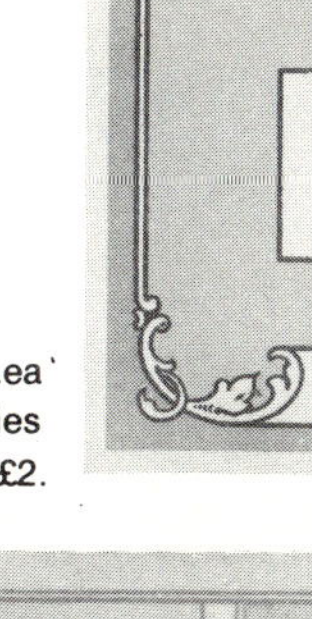

R. & J. Lea' Chairman's Series without imprint – £2.

Suchard Chocolate – Early Vignette – £15

GIVE AWAYS, etc.

These are cards distributed by the advertisers either as "give aways' or in exchange for tokens. Subjects are varied and rarely have any connection with the product advertised. Some firms merely overprinted their blurb or names onto existing cards with or without the publishers' consent!

Amami Shampoo	75☐
Airlines	£1.50☐
Beechams Pills (views)	75☐
Bees Ltd	30☐
Boon's Cocoa (views)	75☐
Bovril (Art Repros)	75☐
Broma Cocoa (Plantation Sketches)	75☐
Butywave Shamppoo (film stars)	£1☐
Cadburys - Butterflies	£1.50☐
Caillers, F. (views)	30☐
Canadian - Dept. of Emigration	£1☐
Capern's Bird Food (birds)	60☐
Carters Seeds	30☐
Chamberlin & Smith	30☐
Chelsea Flower Show	50☐
Chivers & Sons (fruit)	75☐
Clay Cros Co. Mining - Topographical	£1.50☐
Colman's Starch	£1☐
Cook, E. (Aviation interest)	£4☐
Cope's	25☐
Daily Mirror (Beauty Contest)	50☐
Daily Express	50☐
Daily Sketch	75☐
De Beukelaer's Cocoa	50☐
Field, J.	£1.50☐
Fine Arts Pub. Co.	30☐
Fry, J.S. (non-poster)	£4☐
G.P. Govt. Tea (Composite)	£120☐
Garden City Ass.	£1.50☐
Glaxo	£1☐
Goss, W.H.	£4☐
Guinness, A.	£3☐
Guinness, A. Production scenes	£1.50☐
Hadfield, George & Co.	50☐
Hartley, W.P.	75☐
Haydock Coals	30☐
Heinz J. & Co.	£12☐
Horniman's Tea (views)	£1☐
Horniman's Tea (Invisible Picture)	£4☐
Imperial Fine Art Co.	30☐
International Horse Show	£3☐
Jacob, W.	75☐
King Insurance Co. (Kings & Queens)	£4☐
Lemco Coronation Postcards	£15☐
Lemco Cattle (Hassall)	£6☐
Lever Bros. (Port Sunlight)	50☐
Lipton Tea	75☐
Maggi (views)	30☐
Menier	25☐
Mellin's Food	£4☐
Molassine Meal	£2.50☐
Nestles	£1.50☐
New Zealand Tourist Dept.	75☐
New Zealand Lamb	30☐
N. British Rubber Co. (golf)	£5☐
Ocean Accident Corp.	£2☐
Odd Fellows Friendly Society	£4☐
Odol Dentifrice (Actresses)	£1.50☐
Oetzmann's Cottages	£1.50☐
Old Calabar	£1.50☐
Oxo	£4☐
Peark's	75☐
Pears, A. & F. (Bubbles)	30☐
Peek Frean (Invisible Picture)	£4☐
Pertab Sinjh & Zenia Co.	60☐
Phoenix (Poultry Foods)	£6☐
Pickford (Transport)	£10☐

N.B. Have been reprinted

Pitman Health Food Co.	£1☐
Price's Candles (Battle scenes)	£3.50☐
Quaker Oat Smiles	£8☐
Reckitts (Naval)	£4☐
Reeve Jones & Trueman	£1☐
Ridgways Tea	£1☐
Radio Ham (call sign cards)	£1☐
Rowntree	75☐
St. Bartholomew's Hospital	20☐

St. Ivel (views)	40☐
St. Paul's Hospital	20☐
Selfridge Co.	£1.50☐
Shippams	75☐
Singer Sewing Machines	
Aircraft	£3☐
Battle Ships	£1☐
Other types	50☐
Spratt's Dog Food	75☐
Suchard Chocolate –	
Early vignettes	£15☐
Sutton & Sons	40☐
Swallow Raincoats	40☐
Symington & Co. (foreign views)	60☐
Thorley (photo type)	75☐
Trent Pottery	£2.50☐
Van Houten's Cocoa	50☐
Zoo Adverts	50☐
Zoological Society Adverts	60☐

INSERTS

Cards produced by or given away with Newspapers and magazines to woo readers and increase circulation.

Brett' Publications	25☐
Canary & Cage Bird Life	50☐
Christian Novels	20☐
Connoisseur Mag.	30☐
Daily News Wallet Guide	30☐
Dainty Novels	50☐
Captain Magazine (Tom Browne)	£4☐
Christian Novels	20☐
Connoisseur Mag.	30☐
Dainty Novels	50☐
Princess Novels	20☐
Shurey's Pub.	30☐
Sketchy Bits	20☐
Smart Novels	15☐
T.A.T.	75☐
Tiny Tots	75☐
Ward Lock	75☐
Weekly Tale-Teller	20☐
Weekly Telegraph	
(Tom Browne sketches)	£4☐
Weldon's Bazaar	£2.50☐
Yes or No	20☐

REWARD POSTCARDS

Cadbury Bros (Birds)	£2☐
Cadbury Bros (Butterflies)	£2☐
Cadbury Bros (Map cards)	£6☐
Milkmaid Milk	£3.50☐
Nectar Tea	£4☐
Scott's Emulsion	£3.50☐
Hampshire County Council	75☐
London County Council	40☐
Oxfordshire Education Committee	£1☐
School Board for London	£1☐
Surrey Education Committee	50☐

Cadbury Bros. (Birds) Reward Card – £2.

ANIMALS

ANIMALS

Animals - Wild	25☐
Animals - dressed	50☐
Birds	35☐
Butterflies	50☐
Cats	30☐
Cattle (cows etc.)	15☐
Dogs	35☐
Donkeys	35☐
Horses	50☐
Zoo Animals	25☐

ARTISTS

Ackroyd, W.M.	£1.50☐
Ainsley, Anne	50☐
Anders, O.	£2☐
Austin, E.H.S. Barnes-	£3☐
Barnes, A.E.	£1.50☐
Bebb, Rosa	£1☐
Boulanger, Maurice	£1.50-£3☐
Cobbe, B	£1.25☐
Daws, F.T.	£1☐
Donaldini, Jr.	£1.50☐
Drummond, Norah	£1☐
Gear, M	50☐
Green, Roland	50☐
Hayes, Sidney	60☐
Hunt, Edgar	£1☐
Hunter, Mildred C.	75☐
Kaufmann, J.C.	£1☐
Keene, Minnie	30☐
Kennedy, A.E.	£1.50☐
Lester, Adrienne	60☐
Mac	50☐
Maguire, Helena	£1.50☐
Merte, O.	£1.50☐
Nielsen, Vivienne	£1☐
Parker, N.	30☐
Pope, Dorothy T.	£3☐
Rankin, George	£1☐
Reichert, C.	£1☐
Roberts, Violet	£2☐
Scrivener, Maude	£1☐
Sperlich, T.	£1☐
Stokes, G. Vernon	50☐
Thiele, A.	£4☐
Valter, Eugenie M.	75☐
Valter, Florence E.	75☐
Wain, Louis,	
Vignette used*	£8☐
Unused	£12+☐
Later issues	£10☐
Tuck Oilettes	£10☐
Wardle, Arthur	£1☐
Watson, C.M. West	75☐
Wealthy, R.J.	£1☐
West, A.L.	75☐

**used means written on face of card.*

A charming H.M. & Co. embossed card – £3.

Cats in dress, a popular subject – £4.

Cats & Advert, an under-rated Hoffman's starch card – £3.50

An unusual subject from the man who drew comic cats – value £14.

ART (DECO, NOUVEAU AND GLAMOUR)

ART DECO

Artists

Birger	£6□
Brunelleschi	£80□
Busi, Adolfo	£4□
Chiostri	£16□
Cramer, Rie	£12□
French, Annie	£35□
Graf, Marte	£5□
Grosze, Manni	£5□
Grunewald	£5□
Harbour, Jennie	£6□
Hardy, F.	£5□
Koehler, Mela	£18□
Loreley	£8□
Mercer, Joyce	£4□
Meschini, G.	£8□
Montedoro, M.	£15□
Rylander	£6□
Shand, C.E.	£6□
Smith, Jessie Wilcox	£12□
Stenberg, Aina	£8□
Wanke, Alice	£10□
Wennenberg, B.	£8□

Chiostri – a superb example worth more than average at – £20.

Meschini – a nice card of one of the many Deco artists – £8.

ART NOUVEAU

Artists

Basch, Arpad	£80☐
Berthon, P.	£75☐
Boutet, H.	£18☐
Christiansen, Hans	£80☐
Combaz, Gisbert	£70☐
Daniel, Eva	£55☐
Grasset, Eugene	£27☐
Hager, Nini	£25☐
Hohenstein, H.	£10☐
Jozsa, C.	£27☐
King, Jessie M.	£40☐
Kirchner, Raphael (Early)	£50☐
(See also under Glamour)	
Konopa	£18☐
Kosa	£65☐
Kulas, J.V.	£30☐
Larcombe, Ethel	£20☐
Lautrec, Henri de Toulouse-	£300–£500☐
Lessieux, E.L.	£27☐
MacDonald, A.K.	£15+☐
Mataloni, G.	£10☐
Metlicovitz, L.	£10☐
Meunier, Henri	£70☐
Moser, Kolomon	£60☐
Mucha, Alphonse	£80+☐
Noury, Gaston	£30☐
Patella, B.	£15☐
Pinkawa, A.	£25☐
Popini	£20☐
Rossi, J.C.	£30☐
Sonrel, Elisabeth	£28☐
Steinlen, Alexandre	£60☐
Turrian, E.D.	£22☐

Kosa – a major art nouveau artist – catalogue – £65

The Japanese influence from popular publisher, Meissner & Buck. – About £10.

GLAMOUR

Artists

Artist	Price
Abeille, Jack	£16☐
Albertini	£4☐
Asti, Angelo	£1.50☐
Barber, C.W.	£1.50☐
Barribal, L.	£3☐
Bianchi	£3☐
Boileau, Philip	£3☐
Bompard, S.	£4☐
Bottaro, E.	£3.50☐
Bottomley, G.	£1.50☐
Braun, W.	£5☐
Butcher, A.	£1.50☐
Carrere, F.O.	£6☐
Charlet, J.A.	£5☐
Christie, F. Earl	£2☐
Colombo, E.	£3☐
Copping, H.	£2☐
Corbella, T.	£4☐
Diefenbach, K.W.	£8☐
Dufresne, Paul	£3☐
Fabiano, F.	£5☐
Fidler, Alice Luella	£2☐
Fidler, Elsie Catherine	£2☐
Fisher, Harrison	£2.50☐
Fontan, Leo	£6☐
Gayac	£5☐
Gerbault, H.	£4☐
Gibson, C. Dana	£2.50☐
Giglio	£3☐
Guerzonni	£5☐
Gunn, A.	£3☐
Haviland, Frank	£3☐
Herouard	£6☐
Horrell, Charles	£1.50☐
Horsfall, M.	£1.50☐
Horwitz, Helena	£2.50☐
Jarach, A.	£6☐
Kirchner, Raphael	
(Middle period)	£25☐
(Bruton Galleries)	£12☐
(See also Art Nouveau)	
Lasalle, Jean	£2☐
Leonnec, G.	£6☐
Le Munyon, Pearle Fidler	£2☐
M.S.M.	£10☐
Maillick, A.	£2.50☐

Corbella – above average – almost Deco £5.

Marechaux, C.	£3☐
Mauzan, A.	£4☐
Meunier, Suzanne	£8☐
Milliere, M.	£6☐
Monestier, C.	£3☐
Mostyn, Dorothy	£2☐
Mostyn, M.	£2☐
Mouton, G.	£5☐
Naillod, C.S.	£4☐
Nam, J.	£6☐
Nanni, G.	£4☐
Ney	£6☐
Nystrom, Jenny	£4☐
Pannett, R.	£1.50☐
Payne, G.M.	£1.50☐
Peltier, L.	£5☐
Penot, A.	£5☐
Pepin, M.	£5☐
Peras	£5☐
Person, Alice Fidler	£2☐
Quinnell, Cecil W.	£2☐
Rappini	£3☐
Rauh, Ludwig	£10☐
Ribas	£6☐
Rodella, G.	£3☐
Sager, Xavier (Salt Lake)	£6☐
Salmony, G.	£3☐
Schubert, H.	£3☐
Scottie	£4☐
Simonetti, A.M.	£3☐
Somerville, Howard	£3☐
Spurgin, Fred	£2.50☐
Tam, Jean	£6☐
Terzi, A.	£5☐
Underwood, Clarence E.	£2☐
Usabal L.	£3☐
Vallet, L.	£5☐
Wichera, R.R.	£4☐
Wuyts, A.	£4☐
Zandrino, A.	£5☐
Zirka, C.	£4☐

Is this a golfing girl? If so more than £4!

Nice early Tuck
"Art" series - under-rated at £5.

CHILDREN'S CARDS

ARTISTS

Anderson V.C.	£1☐
Alys M.	£1☐
Attwell Mabel Lucie	
Early	£1.50☐
Middle	£1☐
Later	75☐
Azzoni, N.	£1☐
Barber C.W.	75☐
Barham S.	£2☐
Barribal L.	£2☐
Bertiglia, A.	£2.50☐
Bowley, M.	£1☐
Brett, Mollie	£1☐
Brisley N.	50☐
Brundage Frances	£4☐
Caldecott Randolph	60☐
Clapsaddle E.H.	£2☐
Cloke Rene	£1☐
Coleman W.S.	£1.50☐
Colombo E.	£1.50☐

Not usually found as a children's artist – A. Ludovici

Children's Cards published by Liberty & Co are much sought after – £3.50.

Cowham H.	£1.50☐
Dexter Marjorie	50☐
Dinah	30☐
Duncan J. Alan	75☐
Ebner Pauli	£4☐
Feiertag K.	£2☐
Folkard Charles	£2.50☐
Forres Kit	40☐
Fradkin E.	40☐
Gassaway Katherine	£2☐
Gay Cherry	30☐
Goodman Maude	
Chromo – litho	£4☐
Hildersheimer	50☐
Greiner M.	£2.50☐
Grey Mollie	30☐
Hansi	£4☐
Hardy Florence	£2.50☐
Some sets have been remaindered	
Henry Thomas	50☐

James, Ivy Millicent (I.M.J.)	£2☐
Jacobs Helen	£4☐
Kidd, Will	£1.25☐
Kinsella E.P.	£1.50–£5☐
Lambert H.G.C. Marsh	£1.50☐
Lowe, Meta	75☐
Ludovici A.	£3☐
Mair H. Willebeek Le	£4.50☐
Mallet Beatrice	75☐
Mauzan A.	£2☐
Maybank T.	£1☐
Miller Hilda T.	
Liberty	£4☐
Others	£2.50☐
Nash A.A.	£1☐
O'Neill, Rose	£4☐
Outcault R.F.	75☐
Outhwaite Ida Renthoul	£1.50☐
Parkinson Ethel	£3☐
Paterson Vera	75☐
Pearse Susan B.	£2.50☐
Piper George	60☐
Poulbot F.	£2☐
Preston Chloe	£1☐
Purser Phyllis	75☐
Richardson Agnes	£1.50☐
Rose Freda Mabel	30☐
Sowerby Millicent	£3☐
Chromo-Litho	£4.50☐
Sternberg V.W.	75☐
Tarrant Margaret	75☐
Taylor A.	30☐
Tempest D.	75☐
Twelvetrees C.H.	£1.75☐
Upton, Florence	£7☐
Wanke Alice	£5☐
White Brian	30☐
White Flora	£1☐
Wichera, R.R.	£3☐
Wiederseim G.G.	£4☐
Wiederseim G.G.	
Campbells Soup Advert	£30☐
Williams Madge	60☐
Wuyts A.	£3☐

Worth 75p to send today.

OTHER TYPES

Elves/Fairies	40+☐
Nursery Rhymes	£1☐
Photo Type	25☐
School Groups pre-1910	75+☐

TOYS

Bramber Museum (Animals)	75☐
Dolls (Photo close-up)	£1.50☐
Golliwogs	£1.50☐
Greetings Type	30☐
Mirror Grange	£1☐
Queens Dolls' House	£1☐
Queens Dolls' House set	£60☐
Titania's Palace	
Tuck. R.	£1.25☐
Gale & Polden	75☐
Toys (close-ups)	£1.50☐

Tom Browne,
unsigned "Weekly Telegraph" series – £4.

"Scotland the Brave" from Cynicus – £1.25.

COMICS

ARTISTS

A.E.	60☐
Adams, Will	£1.50☐
Anders, O.	£2☐
Austerlitz, E.	£2☐
Bairnsfather, Bruce	£1☐
Bamber, George	75☐
Barnes, G.L.	£1☐
Bee	30☐
Belcher, George	£4☐
Biggar, J.L.	50☐
Bob	£1☐
Boulanger, M	£2☐
Bradshaw, P.V.	£5☐
Broadrick, Jack	75☐
Browne, Tom	
Comic	£2–£3☐
Poster Advt.	£25–£45☐
Weekly Telegraph	£4☐
Captain Mag.	£4☐
Cathedrals, etc.	£2.50☐
Buchanan, Fred	£1.50☐
Bull, Rene	£2.50☐
Buxton, Dudley	75☐
Carey, John	75☐
Carter, Reg	75☐
Carter, Sidney	75☐
Cattley, P.R.	50☐
Chalker	50☐
Chandler, E.	75☐
Christie, G.R. pre 1918	£1.50☐
Christie, G.R. after 1918	£1☐
Colbourne, L.	£1.25☐
Comicus	75☐
Cowham, H.	£1.50☐
Crackerjack	£1.50☐
Crombie, C.M.	£1–£2.50☐
Cynicus	
Court Sized	£6+☐
Early U/B	£1.75☐
"Last Train" etc.	£1.50☐
Later	£1☐
Dauber	£1.50☐
Davey, George	£1.50☐
Dirks, Gus	75☐
Driscoll	30☐
Dudley	30☐

Duncan, Hamish	75☐
Dwiggins, C.V. (Dwig)	£3☐
Earnshaw, H.C.	60☐
Ellam	£1☐
Esmond (Germs Series)	£4☐
F.S.	75☐
F.W.	75☐
FitzPatrick	25☐
Fleury, H.	£1☐
Fuller, Edmund G.	£2.50☐
Gill, Arthur	£2.50☐
Gilmour	50☐
Gilson, T.	75☐
Gladwin, May	£1.50☐
Graeff	75☐
Grimes	50☐
Gillaume, A.	£3☐
Hardy, Dudley	£4☐
Hassall, John	£4☐
Hilton, A.	75☐
Hughes, Lloyd	50☐
Hurst, Hal	£1.50☐
Hyde, Graham	£2☐
Ibbetson, Ernest	£2.50☐
Karaktus	50☐
Kinsella E.P.	£1.50–£5☐
Kyd (See Literary)	
Leete, Alfred	£1.50☐
Lewin, F.G.	75☐
Ludgate	50☐
Ludovici, A.	£2.50☐
Mac	50☐
Macleod, F.	75☐
Mackain, F.	75☐
McGill, Donald	
Early dated	£2.50☐
Pre-1914	£1.50☐
Later	75☐
"New"	10☐
Manavian, V.	£1☐
Martin, L.B.	40☐
Mason, Finch	£1.50☐
Maurice, Reg	75☐
May, Phil "Write Away"	£4☐
Oilette	£2.50☐

A rarely seen Hassall court size "Write-away". Above average and still very cheap at £10.

Meredith, Jack	50☐
Moreland, Arthur	£2☐
Morgan, F.E.	75☐
Nap	75☐
Noble, Ernest	£1☐
Opper, F.	75☐
Outcault, R.F.	£1.50☐
Owen, Will	£3☐
Parlett, Harry	75☐
Parlett, T.	50☐
Payne, G.M.	£1.25☐
Penny, Theo	75☐
Perly	30☐
Pirkis Col	£2.50☐
Pirkis B/W	£1.50☐
Pyp	£2☐
Quinton, Harry	75☐
Reynolds, Frank	£3☐
Right	75☐
Roberts, Violet	£2☐
Robinson, W. Heath	£3☐
Rowland, Ralph	£1☐
Rowntree, Harry	£3☐
Sandford, H.D.	£1.50☐
Schonflug, F.	£3☐
Shaw, W. Stocker	£1☐
Shepheard, G.E.	£1.50☐
Smith, Syd	50☐
Spatz	£1☐
Spurgin, Fred	
(Also Patriotic)	£1.25+☐
Stoddart, R.W.	75☐
Studdy, G.E. "Bonzo"	£2☐
Others	£1.50☐
Syd	75☐
T.B.M.	50☐
Tait	40☐
Taylor, A.	30☐
Tempest, D.	75☐
Thackeray, Lance –	
Write Away Type	£4☐
Oilette Type	£2.50☐
Thiele, A.	£4☐
Thomas, Bert	£1.50☐
Trow	20☐
Wain, Louis	
(See under Animals)	

Phil May by Tom Browne – what more can you say!

One of Lawson Wood's notable "Prehistoric" Series – £2.50 at least.

Ward, Dudley	£1☐
Wilkins, Bob	40☐
Wood, Lawson (Spy)	
Gran'pop	£2☐
"Prehistoric"	£2.50☐
Others	£1.50☐

THEMATIC

Aviation	£1☐
Cats	40☐
Children	30☐
Coons	£1.50☐
Cricket	75–£1.50☐
Cycling	75☐
Dogs	40☐
Erotic	£1.50☐
Football	75☐
Golfing	£1.50+☐
Jewish	£1.50☐
Lavatory	40☐
Local (See Topographical)	
Military	75–£1.50☐
Motoring	75☐
Negro	£1.50☐
Police	50–£1☐
Tennis	75☐
War Comic 1914–1918	75☐
War Comic 1939–1945	£1.50☐
Irish	75☐
Scottish	50☐
Welsh	50☐

WRITE AWAY TYPE

Davidson Bros	£2.50☐
Stewart & Woolfe	£2.50☐
Tuck, R. & Son	
Early U/B	£4☐
Later Issues	£2.50☐

Donald McGill – a postal theme – £2.

A good example from the thematic section, and worth more than the average at £1.

ENTERTAINMENT

CINEMA

Stars

Prices quoted are for **B/W photographs.** *Add half to two-thirds extra for coloured stars.*

Astaire, Fred	£1☐
Bogart, Humphrey	£1.25☐
Chaplin, Charlie	£1.50☐
(Red Letter Stills)	£1.50☐
Dietrich, Marlene	£2☐
Gable, Clark	£1☐
Garbo, Greta	£2.50☐
Harlow, Jean	£2.50☐
Laurel & Hardy	£1.50☐
Lombard, Carole	£1.25☐
Temple, Shirley	£2.50☐
Valentino, Rudolf	£1☐
Wayne, John	£1.50☐
West, Mae	£2☐
Cowboy Stars	£1.50☐
Pre- 1930 Stars	50☐
1930–1950 Stars	75☐
1950's to date Stars	30☐
Film Stills	75☐

"Our Gracie".

"Those were the days" - in Reading? - £4 or more if it's identified.

Miscellaneous

Bioscopes	£4–£6☐
Cinemas	£4–£5☐
Felix the Cat	£2.50☐
Disney Films	£2–£4☐

CIRCUS

Acts	£1.50☐
Adverts - poster type (Barnum & Bailey)	£25☐
Adverts - other type	£8☐
Buffalo Bill's Wild West	£20☐
Animals - caged	50☐
Bands	75☐
Clowns	£1.50☐
Performers	£1☐
Sites (local)	£5☐

"Kismet", a poster ad for one of the Garrick's successes - £5.

Continental advert for "Barnum & Bailey Ltd" - a nice card and well worth £15.

THEATRICAL

Item	Price
Actors/Actresses	20☐
Actors Publicity Photos	30☐
Bernhardt, Sarah	£3☐
Duncan, Isadora	£7–£10☐
Irving Memorial,	£1.50☐
Adverts, Poster type	£5+☐
Artists	
Barribal	£6☐
Browne, T. (Arcadians)	£5☐
Buchel	£5☐
Hassall	£10☐
Kinsella	£6☐
Playbill reproductions	£4☐
Play scenes	£1☐
Amateur Theatrical	25☐
Autographs of known stars	£1.50☐
Ballet stars	£2–£3☐
Ballet Companies	£1☐
Ballet, Modern	50☐
Cabaret	60☐
Concert Parties	40+☐
Conjurers	£3☐
Escapologists	£1.50☐
Gilbert & Sullivan	
Savoy Opera Co.	£2–£3☐
Amateur Performances	£1☐
Magicians	£3☐
Passion Plays (Oberammergau)	25☐
Passion Plays (Oberammergau) (Signed Actors)	50☐
Passion Plays (other)	20☐
Pierrots	40☐
Play Stills, Tuck, R.	35☐
Play Stills, other	25☐
Radio Celebrities	£1.50☐
Speciality Acts	75☐
Stuntmen	£1.50☐
Theatres (close-up)	£2.50+☐
(interior)	£1.50☐
On Piers	30☐
Opera	£1☐

Variety Stars

Item	Price
Chirgwin	£1.50☐
Leno, Dan	£1.50+☐
Little Tich	£2☐
Lloyd, Marie	£3☐
Miller, Max	£1.50☐
Robey, George	£1☐
Tilley, Vesta	£1☐
Others	75☐
Ventriloquists	£2.50☐

The "Garrick", one of London's famous theatres – £2.

Two musical gents – £1.50.

Sauber, a much collected artist.

"The Simple Life" – upper class camping; at £6 probably more than the holiday cost!

ETHNIC & SOCIAL HISTORY

COSTUME

National Dress (Welsh) 75☐
National Dress (Irish) 50☐
National Dress (European) 50☐
Family Portraits 25☐
Family Groups 25☐
Hats 30☐

ETHNIC GROUPS & CHARACTERS

English & Welsh People
(see Rural Life)
Europeans
(see Neudin Catalogue)
Indians 50☐
Irish 75☐
Irish (humour) 50–£1☐
Japanese 30☐
Japanese (art types) 50–£2☐
Scottish 75☐
Scottish (humour) 50–£1.50☐
S. American Indians £1–£1.50☐
N. American Indians £1.50–£3☐
Cowboys £1☐
H. Payne £8☐
J. Innes £2☐
Natives - other countries 50–£1☐

FAIRS/MARKETS

Carnivals £1.50☐
Exhibitions (Local) £1.50☐
Cattle Markets £2–£3☐
Market Places £1.50+☐
Street Markets
(not Petticoat Lane) £2–£3☐
Seaside Fairs £1☐
Street Parades £1.50☐
Travelling Fairs £5–£8☐

FOLKLORE

County Humour 40☐
Customs 30☐
County Sayings 30☐
Dunmow Flitch £1☐
Ducking Stools 30☐
Epitaphs 30☐
Ghosts 25☐
Gretna Green 25☐
Lady Godiva 50☐
Legends 40☐

LANGUAGE

Esperanto (oilette series) £8☐
Esperanto (other types) £2–£5☐
Language of flowers
(Welch, J.) 50☐
Language of fruit 50☐
Language of stamps £2+☐
Language of vegetables
(Valentine series) 50☐
Language of vegetables
(other issues) 50☐

LONDON LIFE

Cries of London
(Rotophot) £1.50☐
Rotary Series £8–£15☐
Sauber £6☐
Tuck, R., Early £8☐
Tuck, R., Oilette £3☐
Others £1–£5☐

MEDICAL

Hospital wards 75☐
Nurses 50–£1.50☐
Operations £1☐
Red Cross Postcards £1.50+☐
St. John's Ambulance 75☐

POLICE

Policemen (single) £1☐
Policemen (groups) £1☐

POSTAL

Early Postman c.1900
Photo type £1.50☐
Later Postman £1☐
Postman with hand cart
(photo type - identified) £3.50☐
Postmen of the World £5☐
Postmen of the British
Empire £4☐
Postmen - Novelty
Pull outs £1.50☐
Post Boxes, etc. £1.50☐
Mail Vans, etc. £2.50☐
Post Offices (see Topographical)

RELIGION

Organisations

Church Army	£1☐
Salvation Army (General Booth/Portraits)	£1☐
Salvation Army (other issues)	£1☐

Miscellaneous

Clergy/Portraits	20☐
Evangelists/Vans	£2☐
Jewish Greetings	£3–£5☐
Lord's Prayer	75☐
Roman Catholicism (Popes/Portraits)	50☐
Roman Catholicism (Popes/Mourning Cards	£3☐
Other Religion	20☐

Missionary Societies

Baptist Missionary Society	40☐
Church Missionary Society	35☐
London Missionary Society	30☐
London Society for Promoting Christianity among the Jews	60☐
Religious Tract Society	30☐
Society for the Propagation of the Gospel	30☐

A spot of gardening, the cabbages look fine – £2

Working on the railway, believed to be in Essex – £3

An interesting Topographical subject card from Brighton – £3.

Self-employed postcard dealer – £1.25.

South American Missionary Soc.	30☐
Universities' Mission to Central Africa	30☐
Other issues (Un-named Societies)	30☐

RURAL LIFE

Blacksmith	£2☐
Bootmaker	£2☐
Cliff Climbers	£1.50☐
Coracle Fishermen	£1.50☐
Children at Play	£1☐
Crofters	75☐
Dalesmen	75☐
Deer Stalking	75☐
Farm workers	75–£1.50☐
Flower farming	£1☐
Flower picking	£1.50☐
Fruit picking	£1.50☐
Gipsies	£2–£4☐
Hop pickers (printed)	£UE—D
Hop pickers (photo)	£2–£4☐
Harvesting	75☐
Herdsman	50☐
Gams (Village	50–£1☐
Hermits	£1.50☐
Lambing	40☐
Lace making	75–£1.50☐
Lavender Fields	75☐
Peat digging	£1+☐
May Day Celebrations	£2☐
Ox Carts	£2+☐
Ploughing	£1.50☐
Reaping	£1☐
Sheep shearing	£1☐
Sheep dip	50☐
Spinning	75☐
Stocks	40☐
Village Crafts	£1–£2☐
Village folk	£1–£2☐
Water Carriers	£1☐
Wheel makers	£3☐
Strawberry pickers	£1.50☐
Village Life – oilette type	£2☐

Although many of the cards listed above will be photographic, superb examples will always fetch considerably more, up to £5 and over not being unusual.

1929 Philatelic Exhibition at Turin – a good example of the Italian cards now found in this country – £12.

Heath Robinson's "Ideal Home." THE DINING ROOM.
Daily Mail Ideal Home Exhibition, OLYMPIA, W., 1934.

Modern Times à la Heath Robinson – £2.50.

EXHIBITIONS

If a postcard has also an exhibition postmark this could increase the price considerably. The prices shown here are for the picture side only.

Exhibition	Price
Nuremberg 1882	£35☐
Paris 1889	£25☐
Columbian 1893	£10☐
Berlin 1896	£10☐
Geneva 1896	£9☐
Nuremberg 1896	£9☐
Brussels 1897	£9☐
Hamburg 1897	£9☐
Leipzig 1897	£9☐
Turin 1898	£5☐
Paris 1900	£3☐
Glasgow 1901	£4☐
Pan-American 1901	£2☐
Cork 1902	£4☐
Wolverhampton 1902	£4☐
Earls Court 1903	£3☐
Highland 1903	£3☐
Bradford 1904	£2☐
Earls Court 1904	£2☐
Nantes 1904	50☐
Pan-Celtic Congress 1904	£1☐
St. Louis 1904	£1.50☐
Earls Court 1905	£1☐
Liege 1905	30☐
Nelson Centennial	50☐
I.R. Austrian 1906	75–£1.50☐
Marseilles 1906	25☐
Milan 1906	30☐
Irish International 1906	£1☐
Jamestown 1907	£1☐
Irish International 1907	£1☐
Liege 1907	20☐
Palestine Exhibition 1907	£1.50☐
Franco-British 1908	20☐
Bradford Exhibition 1908	£1.50☐
Balkan States Exhibition 1908	75☐
Alaska-Yukon-Pacific 1909	75☐
Imperial International 1909	75☐
Brussells 1910	15☐
Canadian National 1910	45☐
Japan British 1910	25☐
Charleroi 1911	20☐
Coronation Exhibition 1911	75☐
Festival of Empire 1911	£1☐
Scottish 1911	£1☐
Turin 1911	20☐
Dusseldorf 1912	20☐
Latin British 1912	75☐
Gand 1913	15☐
Ghent 1913	20☐
Leipzig 1913	20☐
Palestine Exhibition 1913	£1☐
Anglo-American 1914	40☐
Panama-Pacific 1915	50☐
Brussels-Leakin 1919	25☐
Marseilles 1922	20☐
British Empire 1924	50☐
British Empire 1925	£1☐
Paris 1925	40☐
Newcastle-upon-Tyne 1929	£2☐
Antwerp 1930	20☐
Liege 1930	20☐
Paris 1931	20☐
Brussells 1935	20☐
Paris 1937	20☐
Empire 1938	50☐
World's Fair 1939	30☐
Festival of Britain	50☐
World's Fair 1960	30☐

Pageants

Pageant	Price
Bath (photo type)	40☐
Bath (coloured type)	75☐
Bradford	75☐
Bury St. Edmunds	£1☐
Chelsea Historical	75☐
Colchester	50☐
Coventry	30☐
Liverpool	£1☐
National Pageant of Wales	£1☐
Newcastle-on-Tyne	50☐
Oxford	40☐
River Peace	50☐
St. Albans (sepia)	75☐
St. Albans (coloured)	£1.25☐
Warwick (photo)	60☐
Warwick (coloured)	£1☐
Winchester	40☐
Pageant Queens	50☐
Other type	40☐

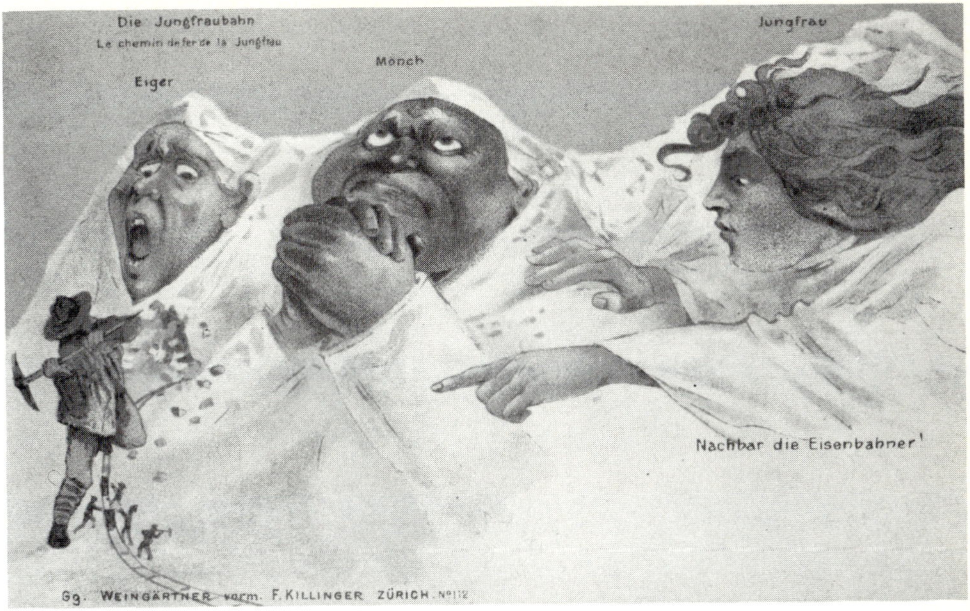

Faces in Mountains by F. Killinger.

Another tall story from N. America for £1.50.

FANTASY

Fantasy Heads B/W	£8–£15☐
Fantasy Heads Col.	£20–£30☐
Faces in Mountains	
Killinger	£15–£25☐
Later Issues	£10–£15☐
Faces in Smoke, etc.	£1.50–£3.50☐
Babies/Children	£1.50☐
Enlarged Objects	£1–£2☐
Maps	£10–£15☐

A rare coloured fantasy head of Lord Byron, must be £30 for these.

A fantasy card from an artist now selling well - C. Dana Gibson - £3.

Pigs & Year Dates – two sought-after types – £6.

The Xmas Mails by the European artist Mailick – about £3.

GREETINGS

FATHER CHRISTMAS

Early embossed	
(Red Robes)	£4+☐
(other col. robes)	£6☐
Non embossed	£1.50–£2.50☐
Photo type	75☐
1st W.W. Silk types	
(See Silk Section)	
Hold to Light Type	
(See Novelty Section)	

GREETINGS TYPES

Birthday/Deckle-edge *c.*1930	10☐
Birthday/other types	10☐
Christmas	15☐
Easter	30☐
Halloween	£2☐
Jewish New Year	£3–£5☐
New Year	20☐

New Year cards have a variety of themes – this one, embossed, would fetch £2–£3.

Popular on the other side of the Atlantic – Father Christmas.

St. Patrick's Day	£2☐
Thanksgiving Day	£2☐
Valentine's Day	£1–£3☐
Embossed/early	£2☐
Embossed/Other types	30☐
Faith, Hope & Charity	
Set of 3	£3–£6☐
Single cards	50–£1☐
Hands across the Sea	40☐
Illuminations	20☐
Maps (Romantic & Comic)	30☐
Moonlight	15☐
Mottoes/Sayings	20☐
Rough Seas	10☐
Silhouettes	75☐
Silks (Embroidered & Woven)	
(See under Silks)	
Sunsets	10☐
Swastikas/Greetings type	30☐
Twenty First Birthday	20☐
Wedding Anniversary	20☐
Wedding Day	20☐

LARGE LETTER

Date cards (embossed type)	£3☐
Year cards (embossed type)	£4–£6☐
Calendar cards	£1–£2☐
Days of the week	50☐
Initials/Alphabet	75–£1.50☐
Initials Tucks "Cherubs"	£4.50☐
Initals/Tucks Complete Sets	£35–£150☐
Names of boys	40+☐
Names of girls	30+☐
Names of places	75☐
Numbers	50–£1.50☐

Hold to Light

See under Novelty

Large Letters and Fantasy Babies – £2 for this one.

This set comes with Continental and Tuck back.
Who came first? – £4.50.

LANGUAGE OF

Flowers (Welch, J.)	75☐
Others	50+☐
Fruit	50☐
Stamps	£2☐
Vegetables (Valentine series)	50☐
Other issues	50☐

PUBLISHERS OF GREETINGS POSTCARDS

We feel that the diversity of most publishers' work makes nonsense of any attempt to quote a price for their cards, except where they fall into other listed categories.

HERALDIC

Prices quoted are for Town names where other types exist. i.e. Counties, Colleges, Houses, etc.

Tuck's 'Heraldic' early	£4–£5□
B. & R.'s Camera Series	75□
E.F.A. Series	£1□
Faulkner, C.W.	50–£1□
F.S.O. Heraldic Series	£1□
Ja-Ja Series	£1□
Jarrold's Series	£1□
Rapid Photo Printing Co.	60□
Valentine's Series	75□
W.E.B.	75□
W.R. & S. (Reliable series)	75□
Miscellaneous	75–£1□

TARTANS

B.B. Tartan view series	30□
B. & R.'s (Arms, Views & Tartans)	35□
B. & R.'s Camera series	20□
Cynicus Co. Tartans	75□
Davinson's Scotch Design series	40□
Ja-Ja Series	£1□
Greetings Tartan design	30□
Johnston, W. & A.K.	
Tartan & Arms series	75□
Others	20□
Ross series	30□
N.B.'s series (Families)	50□
Newman Brothers (View & Tartans)	30□
Philco series (views & Tartans)	30□
Tuck, R. & Sons	
Scottish Clans	£1.50□
Schwerdtfeger, E.A. & Co. (Tartans, views and verse)	25□
W. & K. series (badge & tartan)	£1□
Valentine's Tartan series	50□
Other types	25□

One of several types of Tuck's early numbered "Heraldic" Postcards – £5.

Ja-Ja – the most popular heraldic card, but still somewhat ignored by topographical collectors – £1.

The scene outside the mortuary at Senghenydd at the "Universal" Pit.
Benton 138 George St. Glasgow. 6.

"Universal" Pit. Senghenydd.
The Canary that was carried down the Mine to test the air.
Benton 138 George St. Glasgow. 10.

Welsh Pit Disaster. Lady St. David's visit to the Pit.
Benton 138 George St. Glasgow. 25.

The Welsh Pit Disaster at Senghenydd – £4–£5 each.

INDUSTRIAL

Prices for these categories vary considerably according to area – some being more sought after than others – and photographic cards are considered better than printed.

COAL MINING

Coal Miners – Groups identified	£1.50☐
Coal Miners – Single	75☐
Coal Mines	£2☐
Coal Pithead	£2☐
Coal Mine Disasters	£3–£5☐
Coal Mine Memorium Cards	£6☐
Coal Mine Memorium Gothard	£10+☐
Coal Mining – Art	£1☐
Coal Mining – Exhibitions	75☐
Coal Mining – Wenches	£1–£2☐
Sinking New Colliery	£2☐
Colliery Railway Engines	£2☐
Royal Visits	£2☐
Strikes (Black Leg Marches)	£5☐
Coal Ships	£1☐
Colliery Model Postcards	60☐
Miners Song & Poem (Sets)	£1–£3☐
Underground Views	£2☐
Underground Views (Artist Type)	£1☐
Miners Funerals	£3–£4☐
Mine Rescue Teams	£2–£4☐

INDUSTRIAL

Blast Furnace	£1.50☐
Boat Repairs	£1☐
Factories	£1–£1.50☐
Machine Shops	£1.50☐
Mills	£1.50☐
Cotton (interior)	
" Iron	£1–£1.50☐
" Steel	£1–£1.50☐
" Woollen	£1☐
Mining Copper	£1☐
" Gold	75☐
" Iron	£1☐
" Tin	£1–£1.50☐
Power Houses	75☐
Printing Works	£1–£1.50☐
Royal Mint	40☐

Going . . . going . . .

. . . still going . . . in the Potteries?
– only £2.50 – more if identified.

Tuck's early "Shakespeare" postcard. Far above average at £8.

Dickens characters on Royal Doulton pottery – £5 for the Advertising interest.

LITERARY & MUSIC

LITERARY

Item	Price
Dickens early numbered R. Tuck	£5□
Dickens Postcard Series Tuck, R. "Kyd"	£5□
Dickens Characters Tuck, R.	£2.50□
In Dickens Land Scenes	£1.50□
Tuck, R. Views	£1□
Dickens Sketches	75□
Dickens Houses	20□
Alice in Wonderland	£1.50□
Lorna Doone Series	75□
Poetry (Patience Strong Series)	40□
Poetry (Burns)	25□
Poetry (others)	30□
Shakespeare Tuck, R. Early	£4□
Oilettes Views	40□
Shakespeare (Portraits)	30□

MUSIC

Item	Price
Bands - Dance	£1.50□
Bands - Jazz	£1.50□
Bands - Brass	£1□
Bands - Military	75□
Bandstands	30□
Bells identified	75-£1□
Bell Ringers identified groups	£2□
Champion Bandsmen	60□
Composers Art	£1-50□
Photo	50-75□
Dagenham Girl Pipers	40□
Gramophones Art	75-£1.50□
Photo	50-£1□
Gramophones (comic type)	£1.50□
Hymns	40□
Musical Instruments	20□
Operatic see Entertainment	
Orchestras	60□
Organs - Church (close-up)	35□
Organs - other types (close-up)	75□
Rotary Photo Series Music and Composers	40□
Singers	40□
Singers - Jazz	£1.50□
Music Postcards (Music postcard syndicate)	30□

SONG CARDS

Bamforth Postcards

Item	Price
Song & Hymn Cards In sets of 3	£1-£1.50□
In sets of 4	£1.50-£2□
Odd cards	30□
Black and white odds	30□

Other Types

Item	Price
Davidson Bros.	20□
H.G.L.	20□
Photochrom Co. Ltd	15□
Inter-Art Co.	20□
Philco Pub. Co.	20□
Rapid Photo Co.	25□
Rotary Series	20□
Tuck, R. & Sons (Illustrated song series)	50□
Valentine's Series	20□
Other types	15□

One of Kyd's later Dickens cards - £4.

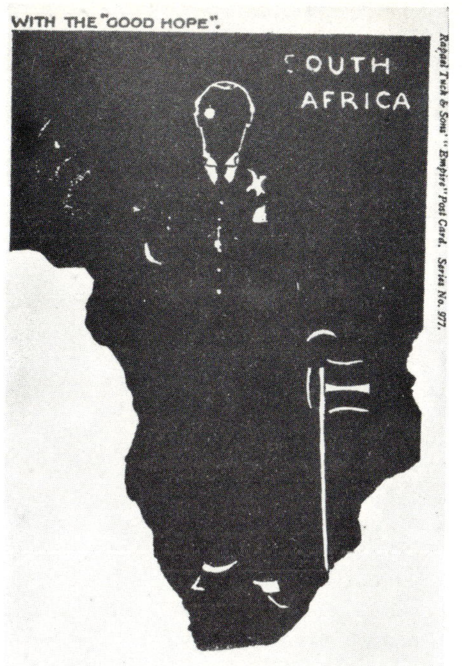

A rare Tuck "Empire" fantasy showing Chamberlain superimposed on S. Africa – £15.

A Russo-Japanese War card celebrating a Japanese Victory – a Better example – £6.

Drinking Victoria's,chocolate! A French view of the Boer War – £8.

MILITARY

BOER WAR

Item	Price
Souvenir of 1900 (Tuck, R. & Sons)	£15☐
Peace Card (Coloured) (Tuck, R. & Sons)	£15☐
Tuck R. & Sons "Empire"	
Col	£10–£15☐
B/W	£8–£10☐
Ships	£8☐
Early Vignettes/Col	£10+☐
B/W	£8☐
Overprinted for Victories	£20☐
C.I.V./b/w Vignettes (City Press)	£6☐
War Sketches	£8☐
European Cards (views)	£4–£6☐
Cartoons B/W	£10☐
Cartoons Col.	£10–£15☐

BOXER REBELLION 1900

Item	Price
War Photographs	£5–£10☐

A rare recruiting poster – £25.

RUSSO-JAPANESE WAR 1905

Item	Price
War Photographs (Government issued)	£4☐
War Photographs (others)	£2.50☐
War Sketches (War Series/Hildesheimer, S.)	£1.50☐
War Sketches	£2–£4☐

CHINESE CIVIL WAR 1912

Item	Price
War Photographs	£3☐

WORLD WAR 1

Item	Price
Allied Occupation/ Germany 1919	75☐
Campaign Maps	£2+☐
Cemeteries	10☐
Christmas Cards (1st War)	£1☐
Dardanelles Campaign	50☐
Mesopotamia Campaign	50☐
Memorials	10☐
Palestine Campaign	£1.25☐
Recruiting Posters	£25☐
Salonika Campaign	20☐
Shell Damage/G.B.	£1.50☐
Shell Damage/Foreign	10☐
Tanks	50☐
Victory Parades/G.B.	50☐
Local Parades	£2☐
Victory Parades/Foreign	30☐
War Wounded	20☐

Other Types

Item	Price
Allied German Camps (Photo type)	£1☐
Allied German Camps (Art type)	£3☐
German Camps	£1☐
Great Britain (Lord Kitchener) Memorial Cards)	£2.50☐
Lord Kitchener	75–£1☐
Other Military Persons (Gt. Britain)	40☐
Other Military Persons (German)	50☐
Other Military Persons (French)	40☐
Other Military Persons (Other Countries)	40☐
Military Art Type Postcards (except listed artist)	75–£1.50☐

Miscellaneous

Army Camps/Fields	75☐
Army Camps/Huts	75☐
Army Camps/Barracks	50☐
Army Camps/General scenes	30☐
Artillery	40☐
Beefeaters	20☐
British in India	30☐
History & Traditions (Gale & Polden)	£3☐
History & Traditions Rates of Pay cards	£10☐
Regimental Badges (G & P)	£2☐
(remainders of **some** *of these have been found)*	
Life in the Army (Gale & Polden)	40☐
Life in the Army (Star Series)	40☐
Life in the Army (other types)	30☐
Medals/Rees, H. (Present Day War Ribbons)	£2☐
Medals (Daring Deeds)	£1☐
Medals/V.C. Winners (other types)	£2–£5☐
Military Tattoos (Aldershot)	30☐
Military Tattoos/Displays (Royal Tournament)	60☐
Military Tattoos/Displays (others)	40☐
Regimental Photographs	30☐
Special Interest (visits, etc)	£1.50☐
Belgian Relief Fund	50☐
British Ambulance Committee	50☐
British Committee of the French Red Cross	£1☐
British Gifts for Belgian Soldiers	50☐

War Photographs/Sketches

Daily Mail Battle Pictures	40☐
Daily Mirror	40☐
Imperial War Museum	30☐
Regent Publishing Co. (The War Series)	40☐
Sketch, The	50☐
Sphere, The	75☐

A Patriotic card from the Australians displaying National Flag & Emblems. £3 for the overseas interest.

PATRIOTIC

Art Type	£1–£3☐
Boer War see above	
Bull Dogs	50☐
Church type	50☐
Comic type	£1–£2☐
Greetings type	50☐
Flags	£1.50☐
Nelson type	50☐
Poem type	75☐
Punch (issued by)	£1☐
Royalty type	£1☐
Romantic type	25☐
Soldiers verse	40☐
Thanksgiving	50☐
Uniforms (sepia-coloured)	30☐

SPANISH CIVIL WAR 1935	£5-£10☐
ABYSSINIAN WAR 1939	**£4**☐

WORLD WAR II

Germany Nazi issues	£4-£10☐
Great Britain Bomb Damage	£1+☐
Comics	£2☐
Leaders	£1-£2☐
Churchill	£2-£4☐
Netherlands	
Cartoons anti-Nazi	£6☐
Comics	£1.50-£2☐
Leaders (Allied)	£1-£2☐
U.S.A.	
Comic and Patriotic	75-£1.50☐

MILITARY ARTISTS

Bairnsfather, B.	£1☐
Baker Granville H.	£3☐
Becker C.	£5☐
Beraud N.	£3☐
Bourillon	£2☐
Dupuis Emil	£4☐
Hardy, F.C.	£1.50☐
Henckle Carl.	£4☐
Holloway Edgar H.	£2☐
Hudson, Gerald	£2☐
Ibbetson, Ernest	£3☐
Leigh, Conrad	50☐
McNeill J.	£8☐
O'Bierne F.	£8☐
Payne, Harry	
Tuck Vignette	£10☐
Empire	£10-£15☐
Oilette	£2-£4☐
N.B. Some rarer series are worth up to £10 each.	
Badges & Wearers	£7☐
Defenders	£5☐
Stewart & Wolf	£6☐
Hildersheimer	£6☐
Simkin R.	£8☐
Stewart J.A.	£2.50☐
Toussaint M.	£4☐
Ward Herbert	£2.50☐
Woodville R.Caton	£2☐

W.W.2 Dutch caricature of "Monty" - £2.50.

Harry Payne - Badges & Their Wearers - £7.

Circular Quay (West Side), Sydney.

Embossed 'Stamp' card of New South Wales. Worth £5 plus £2 for the additional inset picture.

"Good Cheer!" It comes from
the Sunny South,
And is wafted far over the sea;
And it tells you that, under the Southern Cross,
Someone is thinking of thee.

Away in the land of the Wattle
and Gum,
And the home of the Kangaroo,
'Tis there, where the Laughing Jack
laughs all day,
There is somebody thinking of you.

Reg. Copyright. No. 16

Lead applique figure of a Kangaroo – Worth £2.50.

NOVELTY

APPLIQUE TYPES

Dried flowers	£1☐
Feathered Birds (real feathers)	£6–£10☐
Feathered Hats	£4☐
Jewels	£1☐
Metal Models (cars etc.)	£2.50☐
Real Hair	£6–£8☐
Sand Paper (Match Strikers)	£2–£3☐
Sand Pictures	£2☐
Sand pictures (Isle of Wight)	£3☐
Velvet	£1.50☐
Other types	75☐

COIN

National (embossed)	£5☐
National (printed)	£4☐
Coin Greetings Type	£3☐
Banknotes	£4–£6☐

COMPOSITE SETS

Large 10–12 cards (Napoleon, Christ, Jean D'Arc, etc)	£40–£60☐
Early European Sets 3-5 cards (usually animals)	£30–£50☐
American Sets	£20–£35☐
G.P. Govt. Tea (Edward VII)	£120☐

HOLD-TO-LIGHT

Continental	£6☐
Exhibitions	£6☐
G.B. Views (cut-out type)	£3☐
Greetings (Father Xmas)	£7–£8☐
Greetings (Others)	£5☐

MECHANICAL TYPES

Blow out type	£5☐
Kaleidoscopes	£20☐
Lever change type	£3☐
Moveable hats	£3☐
Paper chains	£15–£20☐
Venetian Blinds	£3☐
Roller Blinds (early)	£30☐
Rotating types	£5–£10☐
Stand up types	£5☐
Other types	£1.50☐

PULL-OUT TYPE

Artist (Mabel Lucie Attwell etc)	£1.50☐
Animals (wild)	50☐
Bottles of Beer	£1☐
Bus	£1.50☐
Cars (motor)	£1.50☐
Cats	75☐
Comic	50☐
Coronation Souvenir	£2.50☐
Dogs	60☐
Fortune Telling	£1.50☐
Irish Shamrocks etc.	£2☐
Maps	75☐
Military type (camps)	£1.50☐
Military type (soldiers)	75☐
Military type (other)	75☐
Postman	£2☐
Products (Tins of salmon etc.)	£1☐
Railway Tickets (Town Names)	£1☐
Rural scenes (Kent hop fields etc.)	£2☐
Ships	£1.50☐
Town Names	£1☐
Trams	£2☐
Valentine (Heraldic type)	£1.50☐
Views of towns (multi-view fronts)	75☐
Welsh Ladies	£1☐

STAMP CARDS

Embossed (Zieher, O.)	£5□
Embossed USA (Zieher, O.)	£10□
Embossed (other publishers)	£5□
Printed (Zieher, O.)	£4□
Other Publishers	£4□
Black & White Printed	£2□
Modern (Robson Lowe Ltd)	50□

TRANSPARENCIES

Continental	£8□
Exhibitions	£10–£15□
G.B. views (Col. change)	£3□
G.B. views Meteor Type. Pub. by Hartmann	£7□
Greetings (Father Xmas)	£6–£8□
Greetings (Others)	£4–£6□
Meteors	£10□
Puzzle Type	£4□

MISCELLANEOUS

Aluminium	£2□
Bas Relief	£1□
Book mark types	50□
Celluloid	£2□
Celluloid - embossed (very rare)	£6□
Cut-out models	£6–£10□
Glass eyes (cats etc.)	£1.50□
Glitter type	30□
Gramophone Records Tuck, R.	£4□
Gramophone Records (early type)	£10□
Gramophone Records (other types)	£5□
Invisible picture type (coin rub)	£3□
Jigsaw puzzles (Tuck, R.)	£12□
Jigsaw puzzles (other types)	£10□
Leather	£2.50□
Midget type	50□
Mirror type	£1□
Panel type	30□
Peat type (real Irish)	£3□
Perfumed	£1.50□
Photo inset - seaside	50□
Puzzle type	£2□
Shapes	£2 £10□
Squeakers	£2□
3D types (complete with eye piece)	£4□
Unusual sizes (all other than listed)	£1□
Wood	£2□

Shapes - Puss in Boots - address label printed on reverse - £9.

OVERSEAS

As this is a new section on a subject previously unlisted, we have pitched the prices at the level you would expect to pay from a dealer who had a market for this type of card, but not the specialist, mainly philatelic, buyers who exist and would, in some cases, pay more.

At the moment only slight notice is taken of whether a card is a street scene, or just scenery, particularly for the scarcer countries, but the street scenes sell better. Ethnic cards can, of course, fetch more.

European cards: Prices given are for G.B. market and for further information see appropriate overseas catalogues in Bibliography. European countries omitted are those of which we have no knowledge at the present time.

Aden*	30
Antigua*	£1
Ascension**	£4
Australia (Street scenes)	75–£1
Australia (Others)	40
Bahamas*	60
Bahamas (American Coloured type)	40
Barbados*	60
Basutoland*	50
Belgium Streets and Villages	£1-£2
Bermuda*	60
Bolivia	40
Brazil	45
British Guiana	50
British Honduras	50
Burma	60
Canada - Patriotic (embossed)	£2.50
Canada - Souvenir	£1.50
Canada - Street Scenes	40–75
Ceylon	20
Chile	40
China*	40
Cuba	30
Cyprus*	60
Czechoslavakia	10
Danish W. Indies*	50
Denmark (streets)	75
Dominica*	75
Egypt	25
Estonia	60
Falkland Islands**	£10
Falkland Islands Penguins and Birds**	£8
Fiji*	75
Finland (Street Scenes)	£1
French Colonies*	20-£1
France (Street scenes)	50-75
Germany	50-£1
Gibraltar*	25-40
Gilbert and Ellice I.**	£5
Greece	40
Grenada (G.B. Colony)*	60
Hong King*	40-60
Hungary	40
Iceland	75
India	20-30
Jamaica*	50
Japan	20
Labuan**	£2
Lagos*	75
Latvia	75
Leeward Islands*	75
Lithania	60
Malaya	40-60
Malta*	30-40
Mauritius*	75
Mexico	40
Montserrat* (G.B.)	75
New Guinea*	£2
New Hebrides*	£2
N. Zealand	40-75
Nigeria	50
Norfolk Islands**	£5
North Borneo*	£2
Norway	30-£1
Palestine*	20-40
Panama	25
Papua*	£2

Persia	75
Pitcairn Island**	£5
Rhodesia*	40–60
Romania	50
Russia*	25–75
St. Helena*	£1.50
St. Kitts*	75
St. Lucia*	75
St. Vincent*	£2
Samoa*	£2
Sarawak*	£2
Seychelles*	£5
Sierra Leone	40
Solomon Islands**	£3
South Africa	40–75
Sweden	50–£1
Switzerland	25–50
Tonga*	£2
Trinidad*	75
U.S.A.	25–60
Zanzibar*	50–75

Life up a tree – Malayan Style! – Worth 75p.

Ascension – Doesn't look very much, but keenly sought after.

* Indicates that, if postally used in the place of origin they are possibly worth more.
Indicates **definitely worth much more.

POLITICAL

CARTOONS

Item	Price
Dreyfus 1899	£6–£8☐
Alsace Lorraine 1903	£6☐
Bulgaria 1903	£6☐
Irish Home Rule 1912	£5☐

N.B. See also MILITARY Section.

World War 1 1914–1918

Item	Price
Edith Cavell - Mourning Cards	£2☐
France (Les Monstres des Cathedrales)	£4☐
France (other issues)	£1.50☐
Germany	£2.50☐
Great Britain (Jarrold & Sons 'Punch' Reproductions)	£1.50☐
Great Britain Tuck, R. & Sons (Aesop's Fables)	£6☐
Great Britain	£1.50☐
Italy (Sculpture montage)	£2☐
Italy	£1.50☐
Human Butterflies (Pretty Girls/ Statesmen)	£5☐
Raemaeker, Louis	£1.50☐
Other issues	£1.50☐

A common "Home Rule" card – £5.

"Aesop's Fables". The W.W.1 Political situation as seen by Sancha – £6.

World War II £1.50□

SOCIAL

R. Tuck & Sons
Political Postcards £10□
R. Tuck & Sons
Fiscal Series PVB £5□
R. Tuck & Sons
Fiscal Series Others £3.50□
J. Walker & Co. Harry Furniss £4□
Davidson Bros. A. Ludovici £3□
Free Trade £2.50□
Worker's Compensation Acts £2.50□
Suffragette Campaigns £6–£8□
National Insurance Acts £2.50□
Shops Acts £2.50□
Home Rule £6□

Dreyfus Affair £8–£12□

Elections
Canvassing Cards £1.50□
Declarations £2□

Events
Meetings/Treaties £2–£3□
Funerals £1.50□
Visits £2□

Irish Home Rule
Easter Rising 1916 £3.50□
Leaders £5□
Mourning Cards £8□
Ulster Campaign £5□

National Socialist Party £5–£10□

Personalities
Leaders/Statesmen £1–£2□

Suffragette Campaigns
Events £8–£12□
Publicity Cards £10–£15□
Leaders/Portraits £12□

Unrest
Marches £2–£6□
Strikes £6–£10□
Sydney Street Siege 1912 £2.50□

The cause of it all! – £2.50.

A charming suffragette study – £12.

POSTCARD INTEREST

PIONEER POSTCARDS

Official Stationery

Austria

First issue of postcard used October 1st, 1869	£150☐
As above unused	£10☐

Great Britain

First issue of postcard used October 1st, 1870	£150☐
As above unused	£4☐
Penny Postage Jubilee used 1890	£40☐
As above - unused	£20☐
Royal Naval Exhibition (Eddystone Lighthouse) used 1891	£40☐
Gardening & Forestry Exhibition 1893 - used	£50☐
Austrian 25 years Jubilee Postcard showing Dr. Hermann & signed	£250☐

A pre-court sized postcard design in Britain but printed in Germany - Worth £8.

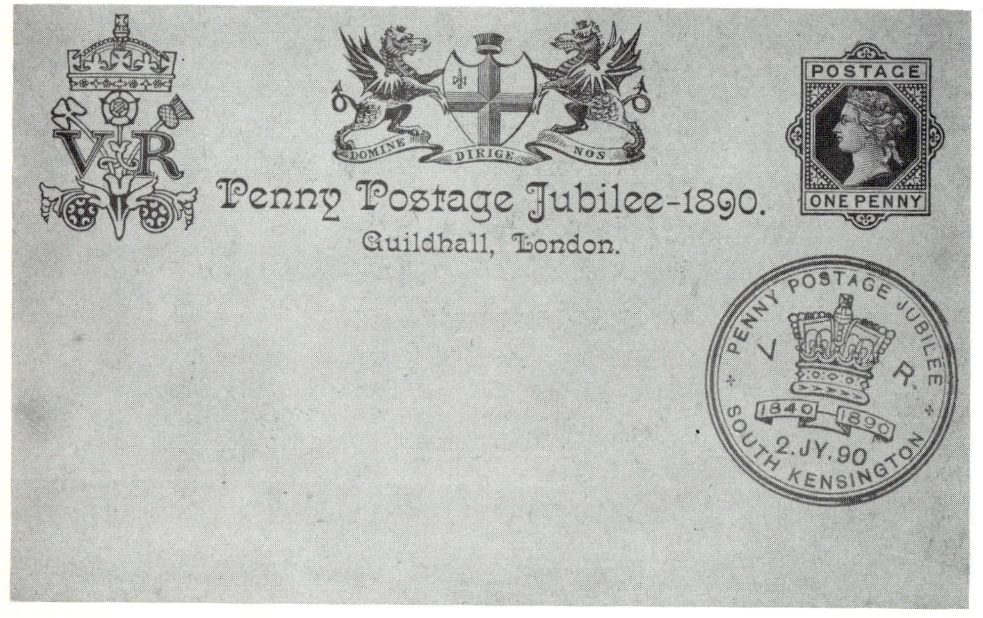

The first British Postcard (of 1890) that is beginning to look pictorial! - Worth £20.

GRUSS AUS FOREIGN

Vignette Views

Col. used	£2☐
Mint	£4☐
B/W	£1.50☐

Used in

1898	£3☐
1897	£4☐
1896	£5☐
1895	£6☐
1894	£8☐
1893	£10☐
1892	£12☐
1891	£15☐
1890	£20☐
Pre 1890	£25–£50☐
Anniversaries	£8–£15☐
Exhibitions	£8–£15☐
Festivals	£10☐
Parades	£10–£12☐
Souvenirs	£8–£15☐
German Colonies	£5–£10☐

An unusual vertical Gruss Aus card from Heilbronn – £3.50.

German Colonies – a charming greeting from Kiaotschau – £8.

GREAT BRITAIN EARLY

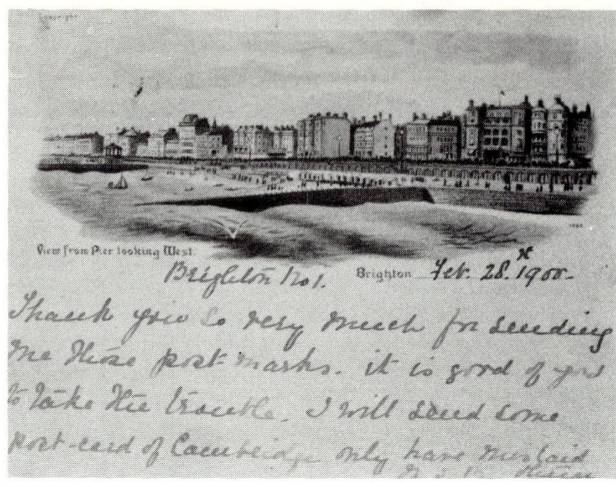

Court Sized becoming more popular and now being collected unused as well – £6.

Court Sized

Gruss Aus type	£8–£10☐
British Colonies	£5–£10☐
Vignettes Col.	£6–£8☐
Vignettes B/W	£5☐

Used in

1898	£8☐
1897	£10☐
1896	£15☐
1895	£25–£50☐
1894	£200+☐

Used cards may be proved as to year by the dated postmark on the Victorian Stamp but the presence of a Victorian Stamp with an indecipherable date is NOT proof that it is pre-1902 because Victorian Stamps were regularly used in 1902, then decreasingly for a year or so later and freak usage is found many years later. As regards UNUSED cards, they are more difficult to allocate to their year and the ability to date can come only with experience, save that 'Court' cards are usually associated with this pre-1902 period.

Intermediate Sized

Vignette B/W	£6☐
Vignette Col.	£8☐

Normal Sized (up to 1902)

Gruss Aus Type	£8☐
Vignette Col.	£1.50–£4☐
Vignette B/W	50–£2☐

N.B. **For used** *see listing above.*

During the year there has been a growth in interest in **early Chromo-Lithographs** by watercolour artists eg Kley, Wielandt, Willi Stower, etc. This is combined with the interest in such early publishers as Meissuner & Buch, Ottmar Zeiher, Willi Stroefer, etc.

Intermediate size card from one of our earliest publishers J. M. Beechings – £8.

Postcard Exhibitions

1898–1899	£75–£150☐
1900–1920	£25–£50☐
1921–1974	£10–£25☐
Modern	£1–£5☐

Modern Postcards

Art Postcards	10☐
Beric Tempest & Co. (Military)	20☐
Carousel Series Limited Edition)	30☐
Centenary of the British Postcard 1970 1st Oct. Used. by B.H.Swallow	£1☐
Centenary of the British Postcard 1970 Pub. by Postcard Assoc.	£1.50☐
General Views, etc.	10☐
London Transport Series	30☐
Milk Race Advertising	50☐
Pamlin Prints	10☐
Salmon, J. Ltd Aircrafts by A.Bannister	15☐
150th Anniversary Railway	50☐
Special Events	50☐
'Stadden' Uniform Pub. by Stamp Publicity Ltd	25☐
Royal Issues	15☐
Photochrom Co.	40☐
Limited Edition Sets (21st Century Club)	£3.50☐

OFFICIAL POST OFFICE PICTURE CARDS (P.H.Q.)

N.B. These issues are mainly collected by Stamp Collectors and therefore tend **to rise (and fall)** *with the stamp market. They must be in* **perfect** *condition.*

1973	Cricket	£30☐
	I.Jones	£20☐
	Parliament	£15☐
	R.Wedding	£2☐
1974	Tree	£50☐
	Fire Service	£30☐
	Britons (4)	£4☐
	Churchill	£1.50☐
1975	Turner	£2.50☐
	Euro Arch (3)	£2.10☐
	Sailing	£2☐
	Railways (4)	£12☐
	Jane Austen (4)	£4.50☐
1976	Pioneers	£2.00☐
	Bicentennial	£2☐
	Roses (4)	£3☐
	Folk Activ. (4)	£1.25☐
	Caxton (4)	£1.25☐
	Christmas (4)	£1☐
1977	Racket Sports (4)	£1.50☐
	Chemistry (4)	£1☐
	S.Jubilee (5)	£2☐
	Heads of Govt.	£1.50☐
	Wildlife (5)	80☐
	Christmas (6)	65☐
1978	Energy (4)	50☐
	Hist. Builds. (4)	40☐
	Coronation (4)	45☐
	Horses (4)	40☐
	Cycling (4)	40☐
	Christmas (4)	40☐
1979	Dogs (4)	50☐
	Flowers (4)	40☐
	Dir. Elects. (4)	40☐
	Horse Racing (4)	40☐
	Year of Child (4)	40☐
	Rowland Hill (4)	40☐

PUBLISHERS

The following list of Publishers is now sought by collectors. Many are numbered and for this reason collectors try and complete the issues of such Publishers. As the price of Topographical cards has risen so much in the past few years it is impossible to give any price range without recoursing to a listing *for each Publisher*, similar to that given in the Topographical section.

- Alphalsa Pub. Co. ☐
- Artistic Stationer Co. ☐
- Bamforth Ltd ☐
- A. & C. Black ☐
- Blum & Degen ☐
- Boots Cash Chemists ☐
- Corkett, F.T. ☐
- Cynicus Pub. Co. ☐
- Davidson Bros ☐
- Dennis & Sons Ltd ☐
- Durie Brown & Co. ☐
- DeLittle, F. & Co. ☐
- Dailey, Max ☐
- Earle Series ☐
- Ettlinger & Co. ☐
- Eyre & Spottiswoode ☐
- Faulkner, C.W. ☐
- F.Frith & Co. ☐
- Gale & Polden Ltd ☐
- Goodall & Sons ☐
- Gosney, C.F. ☐
- Hartmann, G. ☐
- Hildesheimer ☐
- Inter-Art Co. ☐
- Jackson & Sons ☐
- Jarrold & Sons ☐
- Judges Ltd ☐
- Lewis, C. & A.G. ☐
- Longsdorff & Co. ☐
- Lloyd/Aldbury ☐
- London Stereoscopic Co. ☐
- Levy, L. ☐
- Mansell & Co. ☐
- Martin, Charles ☐
- Medici Society ☐
- Meissner & Buch ☐
- Misch & Stock ☐
- Miller & Lang ☐
- Nelson & Sons Ltd ☐
- Nister, Ernest ☐
- Phillimore ☐
- Picture Postcard Co. ☐
- Pictorial Stationery Co. ☐
- Photochom Co. ☐
- Philco Pub. Co. ☐
- Regent Pub. Ltd ☐
- Regal Art Pub. Co. ☐
- Rotary Co. ☐
- Rapid Photo Printing Co. ☐
- Rotophot ☐
- Salmon, J. ☐
- Schwerdtfeger & Co. ☐
- Sharpe, W.N. ☐
- Spalding ☐
- Sturt & Sons ☐
- Stewart, G. & Co. ☐
- Stuart, F.G.O. ☐
- Sborgi ☐
- Steward, Geo. ☐
- Scopes & Co. ☐
- Smith, Gorden E. ☐
- Stewart & Woolf ☐
- Stiebel, Alfred & Son ☐
- Stengel & Co. ☐
- Taunt & Co. ☐
- Tuck, Raphael & Sons ☐
- Valentine & Sons ☐
- Warne, F.W. & Co. ☐
- Welch, J. & Son ☐
- Woolstone Bros ☐
- Wilkinson, R. & Co. ☐
- Wildt & Kray ☐
- Wrench, E. Ltd ☐

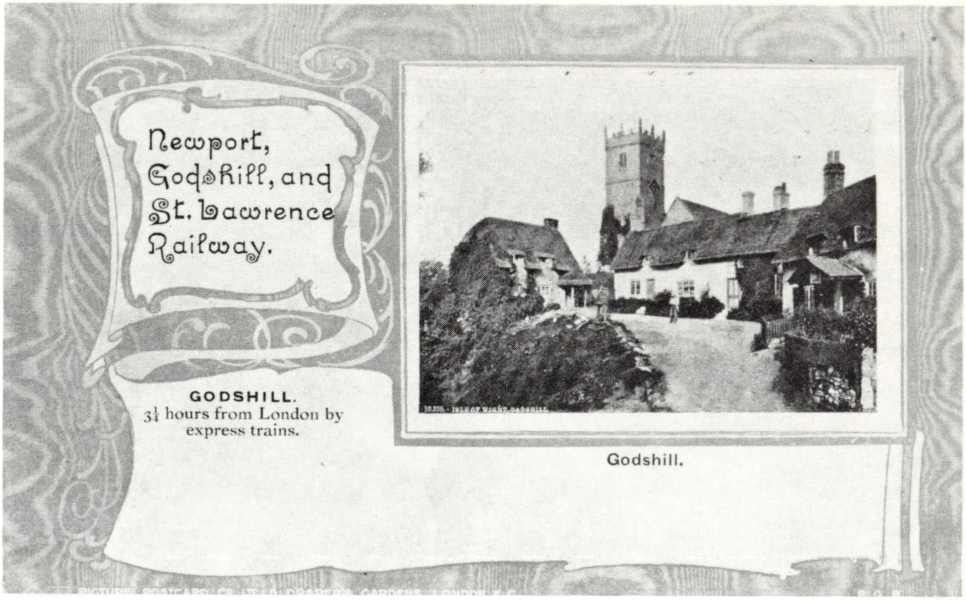
Newport,
Godshill, and
St. Lawrence
Railway.
GODSHILL.
3¼ hours from London by
express trains.
Godshill.

An unusual company, but typical of the small size cards from 1898-9 - £25.

ON CALEDONIAN RAILWAY.
CORRIDOR COMPOSITE BRAKE CARRIAGE.
DINING SALOON (TABLES SET FOR DINNER).

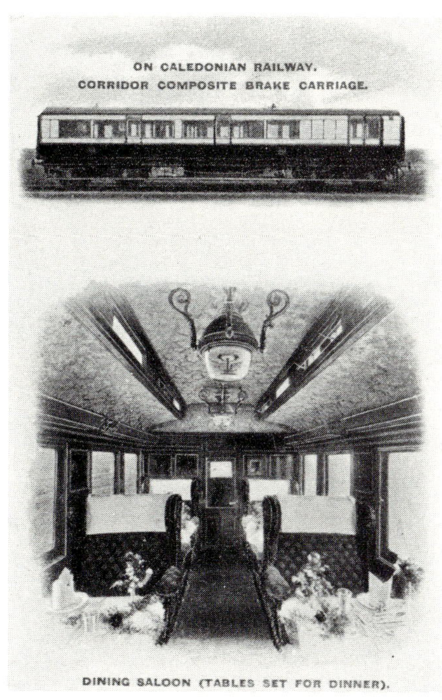

Caledonian Railway. Set 2, 1905 edition - £4.

RAILWAY

Railway Cards fit neatly into three main groups:-

Group 1 - OFFICIAL CARDS

Issued by numerous companies from c. 1895 to the present day. Cards have Company Crests or other official headings on them and are of engines, ships, hotels, views etc.

Group 2 - PUBLISHERS CARDS

Issued by most of the major publishing firms and showing mainly locomotives and trains. These cards were often issued in sets or series and are now once more being produced in increasing numbers by present day publishers.

Group 3 - RAILWAY TOPOGRAPHY

Issued by local/major publishing firms and showing bridges, stations and general railway views. Today these cards are mostly of preserved or private railway scenes. Station issues have almost completely disappeared.

GROUP 1

Early Vignettes (small size)

Cambrian Railways	£25☐
District Railway	£25☐
Great Central Railway	£25☐
Great Northern Railway	£20☐
Great Western Railway	£15☐
Isle of Wight Railway	£25☐
Joint South Western & Brighton Railway	£25☐
London and South Western Railway	£20☐
Newport, Godshill & St. Lawrence Railway	£25☐
South Eastern & Chatham & Dover Railway	£20☐

Early Vignettes (large size)

District Railway	£15☐
Furness Railway (coloured)	£20☐
Glasgow & South Western Railway (coloured)	£20☐
Great Central Railway	£20☐
Great Northern Railway	£20☐
Lancashire & Yorkshire Railway	£20☐
London & South Western Railway	£20☐
London, Brighton & South Coast Railway	£20☐
Midland Railway	£8☐
South Eastern & Chatham & Dover Railway	£8☐

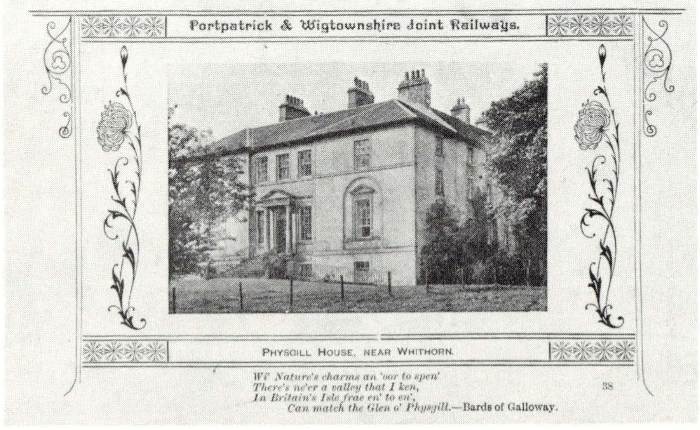

Not an easy company to find although over 100 cards were issued, mostly in 1903 - £10.

Engines/Rolling Stock

Caledonian Railway (coloured/sepia)	£4☐
East Coast Joint Stock	£6☐
Furness Railway (photo)	£2☐
Great Eastern Railway	£1.50☐
Great Northern Railway (coloured)	£1☐
Great Western Railway	£1.50☐
Lancashire & Yorkshire Railway	£1.50☐
Lancashire & Yorkshire Railway (French overprint)	£4.50☐
London, Brighton & South Coast Railway	£2☐
Midland Railway (coloured)	£10☐
Midland Railway (plain)	£2☐
South Eastern & Chatham & Dover Railway (coloured)	£1.50☐
West Coast Joint Stock	£3☐
London, Midland & Scottish Railway	£1☐
London & North Eastern Railway	£1☐
Southern Railway	75☐
British Railways	50☐

Railway Hotels

Caledonian Railway	£2.50☐
Furness Railway (Abbey Hotel)	£1.50☐
Glasgow & South Western Railway (multi-view)	£12☐
Glasgow & South Western Railway (single)	£4☐
Great Central Railway	£2☐
Great Eastern Railway	£1.50–£2☐
Great Northern Railway	£1.50☐
Great North of Scotland Railway (single/multi-view)	£5–£10☐
Great Southern & Western Railway	£6☐
Great Western Railway	£2+☐
Midland Railway (vignette)	£12☐
North British Railway	£4☐
North Eastern Railway	£1.50☐
London, Midland & Scottish Railway	£1+☐
London & North Eastern Railway	£7.50☐
British Railways	50☐

This one will be listed next year – £35.

A good Hotel card, including the Station Hotel, Aberdeen, which opened c.1910 – £10.

Ships and Steamers

Caledonian Railway (Clyde Coast)	£4.50☐
Cork Blackroch & Passage	£25☐
Furness Railway (Lakes)	£1.50☐
Furness Railway (Morecambe Bay)	£5☐
Glasgow and South Western Railway	£1.50☐
Great Central Railway	£8☐
Great Eastern Railway	£2☐
Great Western Railway	£2☐
Lancashire & Yorkshire Railway	£4☐
(French overprint)	£6☐
London & South Western Railway (vignettes)	£25☐
Midland Railway	£12☐
North British Railway	£5☐
North Eastern Railway	£10☐
London, Midland & Scottish Railway	£2☐
South Eastern & Chatham Railway	£1.50☐
British Railways (photo)	50☐
British Railways (coloured)	30☐

View Cards

Caledonian Railway (col/plain, many styles)	£4☐
Callander & Oban Railway	£10☐
Cambrian Railways (coloured)	£4☐
Cheshire Lines Committee	£25☐
Cork, Brandon & S. C. Railway (Oilettes)	£3.50☐
Dublin, Wicklow & Wexford Railway	£10☐
East Coast Joint Stock	£8☐
Furness Railway (Mc Corquodale)	£1.50☐
Furness Railway (Tucks coloured/photo)	£1.50☐
Glasgow & South Western Railway (Oilettes)	£4☐
Great Central Railway (coloured/photo)	£2.50☐
Great Eastern Railway (coloured)	£2☐
(black & white)	£2.50☐
Great Northern Railway	£2.50☐
Great North of Scotland Railway	£6☐

Narrow gauge on the Welsh border – £5.

Great Southern & Western Railway (Oilettes) £3.50□
Great Western Railway (collotype, photo, coloured) £1.50+□
Highland Railway £8□
Hull & Barnsley Railway £10□
Invergarry & Fort Augustus Railway £15□
Lancashire & Yorkshire Railway (coloured/plain) £1.50□
(French overprint) £4.50□
London, Brighton & South Coast Railway £2.50□
Midland Railway £1.50□
North British Railway (coloured/plain) £3–£5□
North Eastern Railway (panoramic) £8□
North Staffordshire Railway (collotype/plain/ coloured) £2–£4□
Portpatrick & Wigtownshire Joint Railway £10□
Welsh Highland Railway £10□
West Coast Joint Stock £6□
Wick & Lybster Railway £10□
London, Midland & Scottish Railway £1□

General Interest Cards

Furness Railway (Art Studies) £1.50□
Great Central Railway (Immingham Docks) £4□
Great North of Scotland Railway (Golfing) £4□
Great Western Railway £1.50+□
London, Brighton & South Coast Railway £2+□
Camping Coaches (LMS & LNER) £1.50□
Exhibition Stands (Various railways except L. & NWR) £4□

Poster Cards

Furness Railway £35+□
Glasgow & South Western Railway £40+□
Great Eastern Railway £30+□
Great Northern Railway £35+□
Great Western Railway £35+□
Lancashire & Yorkshire Railway £40+□
London, Brighton & South Coast Railway £40+□
Midland Railway £35+□
North Eastern Railway £40□
South Eastern & Chatham & Dover Railway £40□
London Underground Railways £12–£35□

Advert/Map Cards

Caledonian Railway £25□
Great Central Railway (Dining Cars) £15□
Midland Railway (map) £12–£15□
South Eastern & Chatham Railway (map) £15□

An attractive LNWR Tuck card from 1904 – £3.

Correspondence Cards

It was usual for railways to use their ordinary series/set cards for this purpose. Many companies issued and used specially produced cards.

Cheshire Lines Committee £25☐
Great Eastern Railway £4☐
Great Northern Railway £4☐
Great Western Railway (Wyndhams) £4☐

London and North Western Railway

Of all the railways in the British Isles, the L. & N.W.R. promoted the picture postcard more than any other company. Some 60 sets of cards (issued on a number of occasions) together with many single cards were issued. Below are given a number of general headings giving an approximate guide to prices. For details of each card issued and its valuation within the framework of prices herewith, see Official Railway Postcards of the British Isles - Part 1.

St. Louis Exposition (U.S.A.) £12☐
Tuck Cards (Engines, Rolling Stock, Hotels, Ships) £1-£3☐
Tuck Cards (Views) £1.50☐
McCorquodale (Engines, Rolling Stock, Ships) £1-£3☐
McCorquodale (Views, General Interest) 75-£2☐
McCorquodale Buses (motor/horse) (lorries/motor transport) £8☐
McCorquodale (Menu cards) £3☐
McCorquodale (Poster cards) £35☐
McCorquodale (Poster ships) £8☐
McCorquodale (Exhibition cards) £6☐
McCorquodale (Hotel cards) (coloured/plain) £2.50☐
McCorquodale (Map cards) £25+☐

Minor Railway Companies

Bideford, Westward Ho! & Appledore Railway (Rolling stock, Views) £15☐
Campbeltown & Macrihanish (Advert) £25☐
Corris Railway (views) £6☐
Festiniog Railway (poster) £40☐
Kent & East Sussex Railway (Rolling stock, Views) £8☐
Lynton & Barnstaple Railway (Engines, Stations, Views) £2-£4☐
Snowdon Mountain Railway (Views) £2-£4☐

The only Rutland station in the extensive Kingsway series. A good country station view - £6.

Electric Railways

Central London Railway	£12☐
District Railway	£6☐
London Transport (Rolling Stock)	50☐
London Transport (Poster cards)	20☐
L.U.E.R./Hampstead Tube - Last Link	£8☐
L.U.E.R./Hampstead Tube - Miscellaneous	£8☐
Metropolitan Railway (Views)	£8☐
Metropolitan Railway (Correspondence cards)	£4☐
Metropolitan Railway (Map cards)	£20☐

GROUP 2 - PUBLISHERS CARDS

Trains & Engines/Pre-1923

Fleury, H	£1.50☐
Knight Series	£2☐
Locomotive Publishing Co. (coloured)	£1-£2☐
Locomotive Publishing Co. (miscellaneous issues)	50-£1☐
Misch & Co. - Noted Trains	£4☐
Moore, F.	75☐
Parsons, F.J.	£1☐
Pictorial Centre/Brighton	£2☐
Pouteau, E.	75☐
Railway Photographs	50☐
Smith, G.	£1☐
Tuck, R. & Sons	£1.50-£2.50☐
Valentines Series	£1☐
Wrench Series/Red Border	£2☐
Wrench Series/Miscellaneous	£1☐

Trains & Engines/1923 onwards

Allan, Ian	30-75☐
Chadwick Views	40☐
Dennis	25☐
Dixon, J.A.	25☐
Judges	25☐
Lake, G.H.	25☐
Locomotive Publishing Co.	25☐
Pamlin Prints	10☐
Photochrom Co.	25☐
Pike	25☐
Plaistow Pictorial	10☐
Regent	25☐
Salmon, J.	60☐
Swallow, B.H. (limited to 100 of each)	20☐
Valentine Series	50☐
Miscellaneous Publishers (Modern cards/Reproductions)	25-50☐

Underground Railways

London

Hartmann, F.	£6☐
Locomotive Publishing Co.	£6☐
Rotophot	£6☐
Smith, W.H.	£6☐
Wrench Series	£6☐

Liverpool

Wrench Series	£6☐

One of a small series for the Central London Railway - £12.

Narrow Gauge Railways

Ravenglass & Eskdale Railway	£1.50☐
Romney Hythe & Dymchurch Railway	£1.50☐
Miniature & Pleasure Railways	£1☐
Miscellaneous Narrow Gauge	£1–£2☐

Preservation Groups/Societies

Centenary Celebrations 1925	£1☐
Clapham /York Museums	50☐
National Railway Museum	10☐
Industrial Railways/Engines	50☐
Narrow Gauge	25☐
Preserved Engines	25☐
Rail 150	25☐
Standard Gauge	25☐

GROUP 3 – RAILWAY TOPOGRAPHY

Cable Railways	50☐
Cliff Lifts/Railways	50☐
Mountain Railways – Snowdon	50–£1☐
Pier/Beach Railways – G.B. locations	50–£1☐
Volks Electric Railway	50☐

STATIONS
see TOPOGRAPHICAL section

Miscellaneous

Accidents & Disasters	£4☐
Bridges & Viaducts, Tunnels	40+☐
Level Crossings	£1.50+☐
Permanent Way	75☐
Motor Buses – close-up	£8–£15☐
Mountain Railways	50–£2☐
Lifts (cliff) etc.	50☐
Modern coloured cards	25–50☐

Marylebone station as seen by Charles Martin. An exceptional card – £8.

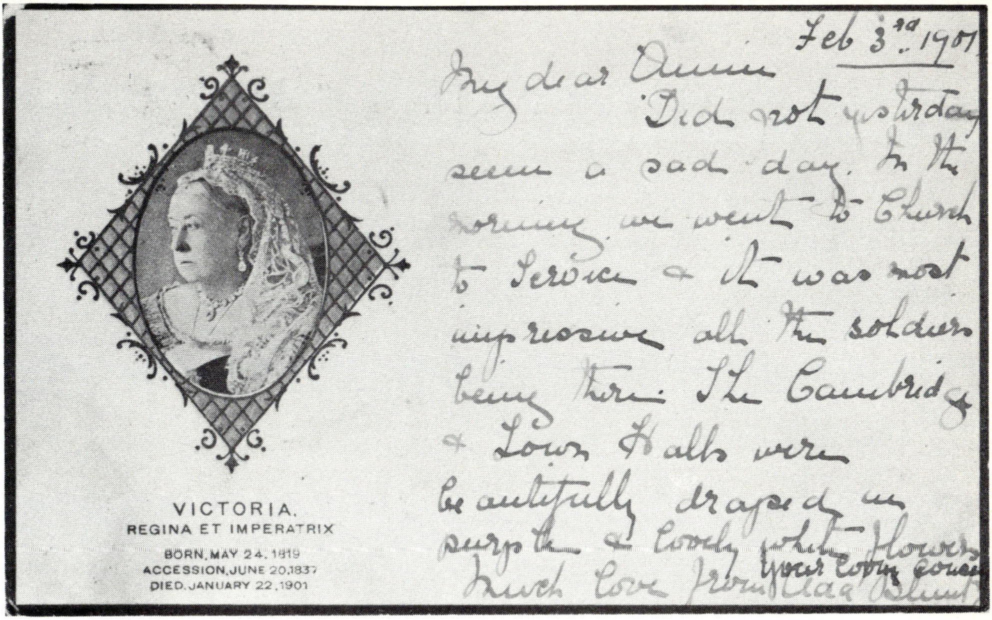

Victoria mourning card from an unknown publisher – £10.

Tuck's "Coronation Souvenir" – from a *Daily Express* drawing – unusual – £8.

ROYALTY

BRITISH ROYALTY

Q. Victoria

Diamond Jubilee 1897 unused	£75☐
used example in 1897	£150+☐
Portraits.	£6☐
Mourning Cards 1901	£10☐

EDWARD VII

Coronation Souvenir 1902	£8☐
Coronation Procession 1902	£1☐
Royal Tour (Tuck)	£8☐
Prince & Princess of Wales	
Others	£6☐
P.U. at all stops set	£250☐
Mourning Cards 1910	£3☐
Funeral Procession 1910	75☐
Visits/G.B.	£2☐
Visits/Foreign	£1+☐

GEORGE V

Coronation Souvenir 1911	£2☐
Coronation Procession 1911	75☐
Investiture of Prince of Wales	£2☐
Silver Jubilee Souvenir 1935	£1.50☐
Silver Jubilee Procession 1935	60☐
Mourning Cards 1936	£2☐
Processions	50☐
Visits G.B.	£1.50☐
Visits Foreign	£1.50+☐

EDWARD VIII

Local Visits 1936	£2☐
Foreign Visits	£2+☐
Coronation Souvenir	£2.50☐
Portraits	£1.50☐

GEORGE VI

Coronation 1937	£1.50☐
Coronation Procession 1937	60☐
Victory Celebrations 1945	75☐
Mourning Cards 1952	£2☐
Local Visits	£1–£2☐
Foreign Visits	£1☐

ELIZABETH II

Coronation 1953	75☐
Processions	35☐
Local Visits 1953	£1☐
Investiture of Prince of Wales	40☐
Portraits Photographic B/W	60☐
Coloured	£1+☐
Foreign Visits	75–£1.50☐
Silver Jubilee Souvenir	25☐

Royal Visits – the opening of the "Old Bailey", 1907 – £2.

MISCELLANEOUS

Royal Weddings	£1☐
Gatherings	75☐

FOREIGN ROYALTY

Portraits

Russian	£4☐
East European	£3.50☐
Others	£1.50–£2.50☐
Embossed Souvenir Cards	£5–£10☐

Foreign Royals – a Montenegran princess in peasant costume – £3.50.

A beautiful example of a coloured embossed German Royal Commemorative card – £10.

SHIPPING

NAVAL

Battleships/Cruisers

Tuck "Empire" Series. Vign.	£8☐
Tuck Oilette Series	£1.50☐
G.B. Types pre-1939 Art type	£1☐
G.B. Types pre-1939 Photo type	75☐
Foreign types pre-1939 Art type	50–£1☐
Foreign types pre-1939 Photo type	50☐
Others (1939 onwards)	30☐
Launchings	£1.50☐

Life in the Navy

Cork, F. (Invicta Series)	30☐
Ettlinger, Max (Life in our Navy)	30☐

"Our Ironclads" one of the Tuck Oilette Series – £1.50.

Chromo-Lithograph vignette of the Royal Yacht by unknown publisher – £8.

Gale & Polden	40☐
G. D. & D. London (Star Series)	30☐
Kelkel Series	30☐
Knight Series	30☐
National Series	50☐
Photochrom Co. (Britain Prepared Series)	40☐
Tuck, R. & Sons (Oilette Series)	75–£1☐
Other photographic types	30☐

Other Naval

Submarines/pre-1939	£1.50☐
Special Interest (Fleet Reviews/ Displays etc.)	75☐
Naval Vessels (Torpedo Boats etc.)	50☐
Sailors photographs etc.	30☐

Lord Nelson Cards

Trafalgar Day Souvenir 1905	£3☐
Life of Nelson/Oilette Series (Tuck, R. & Sons)	£1☐
Life of Nelson/Nelson Series (Gale & Polden)	50☐
Life of Nelson (Woolstone Bros.)	50☐
Life of Nelson (other issues)	40☐
H.M.S. Victory (Gale & Polden)	30☐
H.M.S. Victory (other issues)	20☐

MERCHANT SHIPPING

N.B. Most coloured and some B/W cards were issued by the Shipping Companies and are, therefore, "official Company Publicity" types.

For Woven Silk Ships see **Silks**

Advertising postcards

Poster type (issued by Shipping Lines)	£15☐
Company Publicity type (vign.)	£8–£12☐
Other early issues	£6–£8☐
Later Issues	£2+☐

MERCHANT SHIPS

Lusitania	£2☐
Lusitania (in memoriam cards)	£4☐
Titanic (photo type) Actual	£5☐
Titanic (photo type) "Olympic"	£3☐
In memoriam cards	£6–£8☐
Art type	£3☐
Oilette Series (Tuck, R. & Sons)	£3☐
Other Liners (pre-1939) Col.	£1.50☐
(pre-1939) B/W	£1–£1.50☐
(pre-1939) Photo	£1☐
Other Liners (1939 onwards)	60☐
Launchings	£2.50☐
Interior photographs	50☐
Cargo Boats/Tugs etc.	£1☐
Modern Cards/Reproductions	15☐

Miscellaneous

Accidents/Wrecks G.B. Photo.	£3.50☐
Accidents/Wrecks G.B. Printed	£2.50☐

Company publicity vignette type – £10.

Accidents/Wrecks Foreign	£1☐
Coastguards/Stations	£1☐
Convict Hulks	£2☐
Docks/Harbours	50–£1.50☐
Ferries	75☐
Fishing Industry (Boats/Fishermen etc.)	£1+☐
Historic Vessels (Wooden Walls etc.)	50☐
Houseboats (identified)	75☐
Lifeboats	
Photo	£3.50☐
Printed	£2.50☐
Crews	£2.50☐
Parades	£3☐
"Inland Launchings"	£3.50☐
Lighthouses	75☐
Lightships	£1.50☐
Paddle Steamers/G.B.	£2+☐
Paddle Steamers/Foreign	75☐
Pleasure Boats (identified)	£1☐
Royal Yacht (Victoria and Albert)	£1.50☐
Sailing barges (photo)	£4☐
Sailing barges printed	£1.50☐
Sailing Ships (Photo) (Square Riggers etc.)	£2.50☐
Shipyards	£1+☐
Special Interest (Hull Trawler Outrage)	£1☐
Yachts (River types)	40☐
Yachts (Sea types)	50☐

An interesting steamer publicity card – £10.

Tuck's "Celebrated Liners" showing the work of one of the better artists, so, extra for this – £4.

EAST SURREY
THE
EAST-SURREY

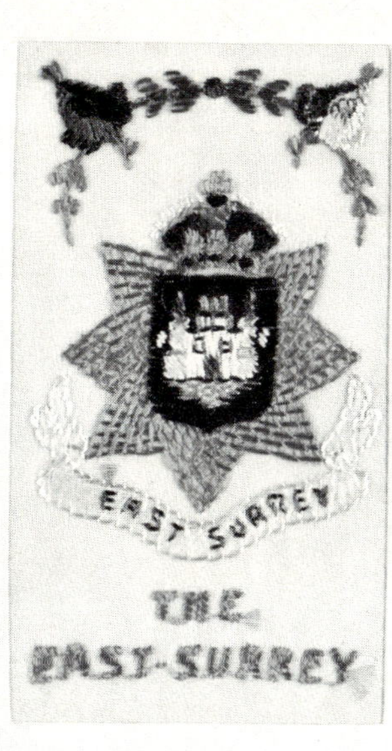

Regimental Badges of W.W.1 embroidered.
The East Surreys - £12.

Mizpah

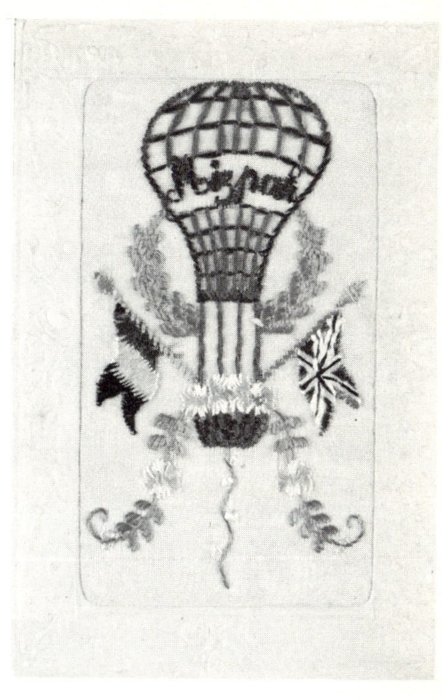

Unusual embroidered design - Balloon with "Mizpah" - £5.

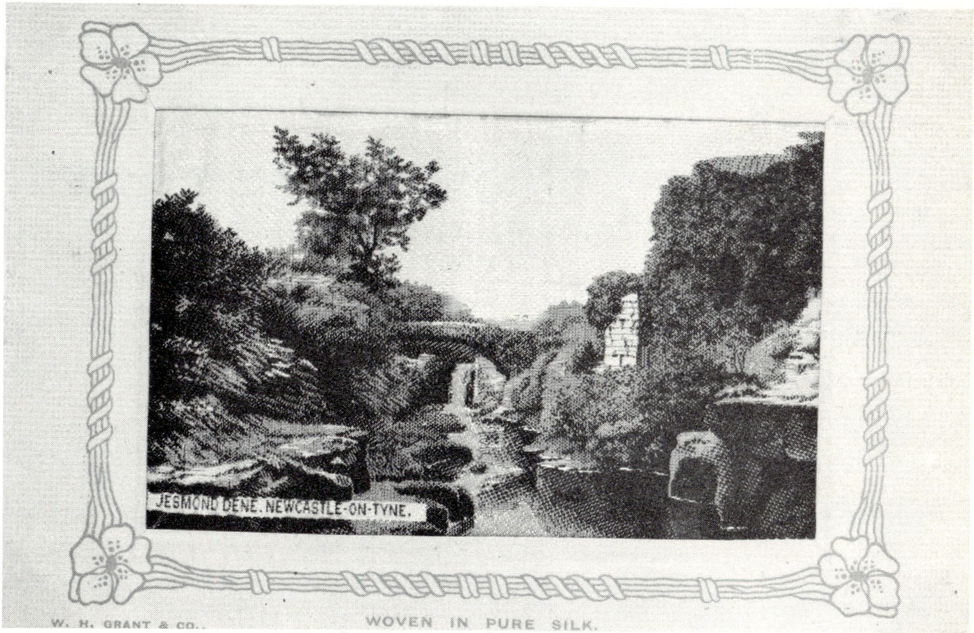
JESMOND DENE. NEWCASTLE-ON-TYNE.
W. H. GRANT & CO.
WOVEN IN PURE SILK.

W.H. Grant & Co. An intricately woven view - £30.

SILKS

This is a vast and complex subject and because of the rarity of some silk postcard designs, it is impossible to quote accurate prices. We have, therefore, used the plus sign (+) to indicate a range of prices with an undefined upper limit. Those needing further information, please see Bibliography.

WOVEN SILKS

W.H. Grant & Co.

Exhibitions £20–£80☐
Portraits £35–£60☐
Ships £25–£50☐
Hands Across the Sea (Ships & Greetings) £30–£60☐
Views £20–£50☐
Subjects £30–£75☐
Greetings (Songs & Hymns) £15–£35☐

Thomas Stevens

Portraits £40+☐
Religious Subjects £35+☐
Views £18–£150☐
Subjects £30–£135☐
Ships
Liners, Steamers & Landing Stages £25–£50☐
Transports £40–£65☐
Battleships £80–£150☐
Hands Across the Sea £15–£60☐

Alpha Series

(Designs produced by Stevens for Alpha Publishing Co.)
Greetings £12–£20☐
Flag Designs £40–£50☐
Stevens Designs £25–£40☐

Early German

H. M. Krieger (Views & subjects) £35–£60☐
Rudolf Knuffman (Portraits Views & Subjects) £40+☐
Other Early German £30+

French

A. Benoiston (Paris Exposition 1900) £50☐

Neyret Freres

1904 Art Nouveau, Classical and portraits £35–£125☐
1906 Views, Portraits & Art Nouveau £35–£100☐
1907–1918 Classical Series £15–£50☐
(N.B. Some of these designs are also found in full col.)
1915–1917 B/W Portraits & Patriotics £15–£50☐
Col. ditto. £25–£45☐
1916–1918 Flames
(Common designs, e.g. Albert, Martyr Ypres, etc.) £12☐
Other Designs £15–£80☐
1917–1918 Greetings £10–£30☐
Bertrand & Boiron
Portraits £30+☐
Other Early European £25–£40☐

Japanese

Views & Portraits £40–£60☐

United States

St. Louis 1904 Exposition £60+☐

Designs Printed on Fabric

Flames – Edition Gabriel £8–£12☐
Edith Cavell (Plain Backs) £1.50☐
Lord Kitchener £6☐
FAB Patchwork
Heraldic Designs £6☐
Views £6–£8☐
Cinema Stars (Plain backs) 75☐
Miscellaneous printed £2☐

EMBROIDERED

Early (Pre-1910) £5–£15☐

WW1

Patriotic (Flags, etc) £3☐
Floral & Sentimental £1.50☐

Regimental Badges

Line Regiments	£12-£15+☐
Corps (ASC, RE, RFA, etc)	£4☐
Royal Navy/RNVR	£10☐
Named Battleships	£25+☐
Royal Air Force/RFC	£10☐
Army Camps	£10-£12☐
Commonwealth Regiments	£15+☐

Personalities

Inset Photos - Single	£8+☐
Inset Photos - Double	£12+☐
Name Embroidered	£15☐

Heraldic

British Towns	£12-£15☐
European Towns/ countries	£5☐
Overseas Towns	£15-£20☐
Overseas Countries	£8-£20☐

Better Designs

Cartoons	£8-£10☐
Views	£5-£6☐
Aircraft, guns, Etc.	£5-£6☐
Salvation Army	£15☐
Santas	£6☐

Year Dates

1914-1919	£5☐
1920-1923	£6☐
1925-1939	£8☐
1940	£4☐
1945	£8☐

Add these amounts to the basic card where applicable

Celluloid Inserts	£1☐
Envelope Type	75☐
Silk Handkerchief	£2.50☐
Inserts - War Scenes	£1.50☐
Perfumed	£1☐
Artist Signed	£1.50☐

Machine Embroidered

Broderie D'Art (R.Tuck)	£3☐
Birn Brothers (These are embossed coloured cards with silk insets)	£3-£8☐
Spanish - Early	£3.50☐
Spanish - Later	75☐

"Flames" a woven silk showing the conflagration at Bapaume - £22.

SPORT

Angling	50☐
Archery	£1☐
Athletics	
Athletes (known)	£1.50☐
Stadiums	£1–£1.50☐
Olympic Games	£4–£10☐
Baseball	40☐
Billiards/Snooker	£1☐
Boxing Amateur	75☐
Boxing Professional	£2☐
Bullfighting Photo	20☐
Bullfighting Art Type	30☐
Cricket	
Players Photo	£3☐
Printed	£2.50☐
Signed	£4☐
Cricket Teams	
Photo	£3☐
Printed	£2.50☐
International	£2.50☐
Grounds	75–£1.50☐

Cup-tie Teams Brighton and West Ham, 1923
£4 for this special card.

Jack Hobbs using his "Force" bat – £3.

Comics	£1+☐
Kinsella	£1.50☐
Cycle racing etc. (see under Transport)	
Football	
Amateur Teams	£1.50+☐
Amateur Grounds	75+☐
Professional Players	£2.50☐
Teams	£3.50☐
Memorium Cards	£6☐
Commemorative Cards	£4☐
Modern	50☐
Crowd Scenes	£1.50☐
Comics	75☐
Kinsella	£1.50☐
Rugby Players	£1.50☐
Rugby Teams	£2.50☐
Golf Players (named)	£3☐
Courses	75–£1.50☐
Comics	£1.50+☐
Product Advert. N.B.R.	£5☐

Tournaments	£2+□
Horse Jumping	
Show Advertising	£3□
Riders	£1□
Horse Racing	
Courses	75+□
Grandstands	75+□
Jockeys	£1.50□
Horses (B/W)	£1□
Horses (Col.)	£1.50□
Hunting Art	50–£1□
Hunting Photo (named)	75□
Motor Sport (see under Transport)	
Mountaineering	25□
Rowing (named)	75□
Shooting Bisley	£1.50+□
Shooting Others	£1+□
Speedway Riders pre-war	£1.50□
Speedway Riders post-war	75□
Swimming Channel	£1.50□
Swimming Misc.	30□
Table Tennis Players	£1.50□
Table Tennis Comics	£1.50+□
Tennis Players	£2.50□
Courts	50□
Kinsella	£2.50□
Walking (Racing)	£1□
Winter Sports	
Skiing	40□
Skating	40□
Tobogganning	40□
Wrestling	£1.50□

A sport not often seen on postcards – £2.

TOPOGRAPHICAL

VILLAGE SCENES	*Photo*	Printed
Animated Main Streets	£3+□	£2+□
Ordinary Street Scenes	£2+□	£1.50+□
Post Offices, Close-up	£4+□	£3.50□
Post Offices, Interiors	£6□	
Post Offices, Middle Distance	£2.50□	£2□
Public Houses	£1.50□	£1.50□
Shop Fronts	£4□	£4□
Local Farms	£1–£1.50□	£1□
Manor Houses	75□	60□
Railway Stations, Interiors	£5□	£5□
Railway Stations, Exteriors	£4□	£4□
Events	£1.50□	£1.50□
Churches and Chapels	40□	30□
TOWNS		
Superb Animated Street Scenes	£5□	
Animated Main Streets	£3.50□	£2.50+□
Other Street Scenes	£2.50□	£2□
Post Offices (Main)	£3.50□	£2.50+□
Post Offices (Sub)	£4+□	£4□
Public Houses	£1.50□	£1□
Hotels	£1□	75□
Shop Fronts	£4□	£4□
Parades of Shops	£3.50+□	£3□
Railway Stations Interiors	£5□	£5□
Railway Stations, Exteriors	£3□	£2.50□
Events	£1.50□	£1+□
Churches and Chapels	40□	30□
MAJOR CITIES/TOWNS		
Including London		
Main Streets and City Centres	30□	20□
Animated Suburban Streets	£3.50□	£2.50□
Side Roads and Streets	£2.50□	£2□
Cathedrals	15□	15□
Church and Chapels, surburban	40□	30□
Events	£1.50+□	£1+□
Post Offices		
Main Exteriors	50□	50□
Suburban	£3.50□	£2.50□
	£5□	£4□

Railway Stations	Photo	Printed
Central Interior	£1.50-£3☐	£1-£3☐
Central Exterior	75-£1.50☐	50-£1☐
Suburban Interior	£5☐	£5☐
Suburban Exterior	£3-£5☐	£3-£5☐
Shop Fronts	£4+☐	£4☐
Hotels	50-£1.50☐	50-£3☐

MISCELLANEOUS

Abbeys	15☐	15☐
Aerial Views	60☐	
Bridges	40+☐	40☐
Castles	40☐	40☐

CINEMAS/BIOSCOPES (see under Entertainment)

Comic (Town names)		75-£1☐
Docks/Harbours	£1☐	75☐
HERALDIC see under		
H.T.L. see under Novelty		
Hotels - early Adverts		£3☐
Hospitals	50+☐	50☐
Markets, Places	£2☐	£1.50☐
Markets, Streets	£3-£4☐	£2.50+☐
Monuments	25☐	25☐
Pull Outs (Town names)		£1☐
Royal Visits	£2☐	£1.50☐
Schools	75-£1☐	75-£1☐

ARTISTS VIEWS for name of Artist see under **ARTIST section**.
As the price of actual Topographical cards rises, these cards are becoming so cheap that there must be a movement towards them.

DISASTERS

Coast Erosion	£1-£1.50☐	75☐
Earthquakes		75☐
Explosions	£3☐	£1.50+☐
Fires	£2.50☐	£1.50☐
Floods	£2+☐	£1.50☐
Lightning Damage	£2.50☐	£1.50☐
Memoriam Disaster Cards	£6☐	£6☐
Memoriam Disaster Cards, Gothards	£10+☐	
Snow Damage	£1.50+☐	£1☐
Storm Damage	£2☐	£1.50☐
Subsidence	£1-£2☐	£1-£2☐
Volcanoes	60☐	30☐
Wrecked Buildings	£3☐	£2☐
Wrecked Piers	£1.50-£3☐	£1-£2☐

For other disaster postcards see under subject headings, e.g. **Industry**.

Farnham – a nice photographic street scene – £2.50.

Of course it's Topographical – The Diver at Winchester – £6.

Crayford, Kent – Lovely village street scene – £2.50.

MAPS

Bacon Excelsior Series	£2.50□
Comic Maps	40□
Cyclists - Touring Club (C.T.C.)	£2.50□
Early Maps	£4□
Embossed type	£3.50□
English Map (P.M. Hope) c.1940	30□
Mountain Tracks (mainly Swiss)	40□
Walkers Geographical Series	£3□

SEASIDE

General Views	15+□
Bathing Huts	40□
Bathing Huts (close-up)	£1-£1.50□
Piers	50-£1□
Donkeys & Children	40□
Punch & Judy Shows	£1-£2□
Sandcastles (photo type)	60□

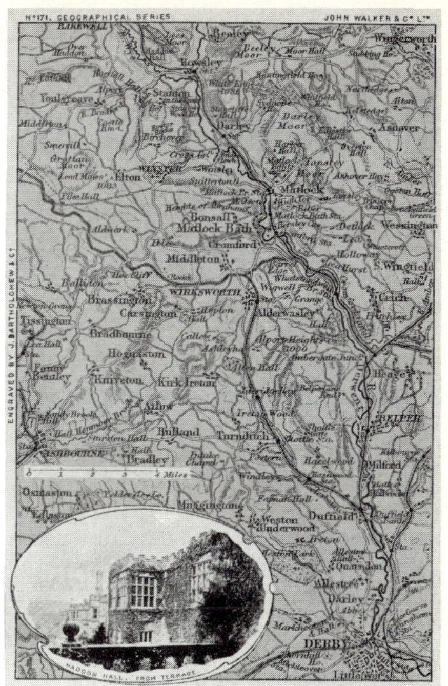

Very much collected now - Walkers Geographical Series - Derbyshire - £3.

	Photo	Printed
WATERMILLS		
Close-up	£2□	£1.50□
Middle Distance	£1□	75□
Art Type		50□
WINDMILLS		
Close-up	£4□	£3□
Middle Distance	£2.50□	£2□
Art Type		75+□
Foreign		£1□
Disasters	£5□	

For **FOREIGN VIEWS** see **OVERSEAS** section. For **TRANSPORT** see under

TRANSPORT

AVIATION

Aircraft

Aviation Meetings,	
Poster Advert B/W	£20☐
Coloured	£30☐
Named Towns	£15☐
Brooklands Aviation	£8☐
Daily Mail Tour 1912	£6+☐
(Aircraft at named localities)	£12☐
Flying at Hendon	£6☐
Pre-1918	
Private	£6☐
Accidents	£8–£12☐
Military	£4☐
Imperial Airways	
Officials	£3.50☐
Pilots	£6☐
Overseas Nat. Airlines	£3.50☐
Art Types	
Tucks, etc.	£4–£6
later, Salmon, etc.	£2☐
Pre-1940	£2–£4☐
W.W.2	50☐
Modern Airlines	£1.50☐
Rockets pre-1939	£1.50☐
Rockets W.W.2	50☐
1950 to date	30+☐

AIRSHIPS

Pre-1918 Military	£8☐
Zeppelins W.W.1	
Combat (Printed)	£2☐
Shot down	£4–£8☐
Civil photo (see note)	£6–£8☐
British R101, etc.	£8☐

MISCELLANEOUS

Airfields	£1–£2☐
Croydon	£2.50☐
Gliding	£1.50☐
Pilots	
Early Aviators	£6–£8☐
Military (Aces)	£6☐
W.W.2.	£3☐

N.B. Used and Flown cards are worth considerably more in most cases.

What can one say about this! £12 slightly damaged.

AMBULANCES

Horse (Photo)	£8☐
Motor (photo)	£2.50☐
Motor (print)	£2☐
Identified	£3.50

BICYCLES

Close-up (photo)	£1.50☐
Advert. Poster	£25☐
Cycling	
Military (photo)	£1.50☐
Social (photo)	£1☐
Racing (photo)	£2+☐

BUSES

Horse, close-up (photo)	£15+☐
Print	£10+☐
Horse, middle-distance (photo)	
Print	£6☐
Motor, close-up (photo)	£15☐
Print	£12+☐
Middle distance (photo)	£10+☐
Print	£8+☐

Street Scenes Local	
Photo	£4-£6☐
Print	£4+☐

CANALS

Aquaducts	
Boats & Barges (close-up)	£2☐
Canal construction/workers	£5+☐
Disasters	£5☐
Feeders	£5☐
Foreign canals	£2.50☐
Inland Waterways Officals	50+☐
(modern)	25☐
Locks and Bridges	£2.50☐
Military Canals	75☐
Narrow canals	£1.50-£2.50☐
Ship Canals	£1-£2☐
Tunnels	£2-£3☐

N.B. Because of scarcity, there is little difference between photographic or printed cards.

A superb lock scene at Tewkesbury. Far above average - £3.

	Photo	Printed
CHARABANCS		
Close-up	£1.50☐	
Middle distance	75☐	
LORRIES		
Close-up (owners identified)	£6☐	
Middle distance	£4☐	
Advertising cards		£6☐
MOTOR CARS (Early)		
Close-up	£3.50☐	£3☐
Middle distance	£2.50☐	£2☐
Advertising		£5+☐
Advertising Poster		£15–£35☐
MOTOR CYCLES (Early)		
Close-up	£3.50☐	£3☐
With sidecar	£4‡☐	£4☐
Advertising	£4☐	£4–£6☐
RACING CARS		
Brooklands	£6–£8☐	£4☐
Peking–Paris		£8☐
Others		£2☐
RACING – MOTOR CYCLES		
Close-up	£4☐	£4☐
Personalities		£1.50–£3.50☐

The club photo. Happy days of no radar traps! Must be worth £6.

TRAMS

	Photo	Printed
Horse Drawn		
Close-up	£15+☐	£12☐
Middle distance	£10☐	£6☐
In Memoriam		£8☐
Steam		
Close-up	£8–£15☐	£6–£12☐
Middle distance	£4–£8☐	£4–£6☐
Street Scenes		£3☐
In Memoriam		£8☐
Electric		
Track Laying		£6☐
B.O.T. Trial Runs	£15☐	£10☐
Opening Ceremonies	£15☐	£12☐
Commemorative cards	£15☐	£12☐
Close-up	£12☐	£10☐
Middle distance		£5☐
Street Scenes		£3☐
Miscellaneous		
Accidents	£10☐	£8+☐
Comic		£1.50☐
Decorative/Illuminated		£4+☐
Terminii (with tram)	£5☐	£4☐
Sheds/Depots	£10☐	£8☐
Works Vehicles	£10–£15☐	
In Memoriam	£10☐	£8☐

FOREIGN it is impossible to price this vast field which depends on the popularity of the Home market, but a *very general* guide would be about two-thirds of the prices above.

	Photo	Printed
TRACTION ENGINES		
Close-up	£8☐	
Middle distance	£5☐	£4☐
Road Scenes	£4☐	£2.50☐
Accidents	£8–£12☐	£6☐
TROLLEY Buses		
Close-up (early)	£8–£12☐	
Street Scenes	£2.50☐	£2☐

Note: These are very rare but little collected.

MODERN TRANSPORT

Pamlin Prints	10☐
Reproductions	15☐

See also **COMIC** section for Transport types.

TUCK, R. & SON

The firm of Tucks have produced more postcards than any other company in the Postcard World. It would require a catalogue larger than this to cover all their issues, so only some of the more collected ones are listed – other Tuck cards will be found listed under subject headings.

It may be of interest to collectors to know that the firm's complete records of their issues were destroyed in the 2nd World War.

Animal Life/Early Vignettes	£5☐
Animal Life/Later issues	£1☐
Animal Studies	30☐
Antique Deckle-Edged Collotype	30☐
Aquarette	40☐
Art/Early Vignettes	£4–£6☐
Art/Middle period	£1☐
Art/Later issues	30☐
Art Collotype	20☐
Art Glosso Greeting	30☐
Bathing Girls	£2☐
Birthday/Middle period	£1.50☐
Birthday/Later issues	30☐
British Navy/Early Vignettes	£6☐
British Sports	£1☐
Broderie d'Art	£3☐
Calendar	£1.50☐
Carbonette	20☐
Celebrities of the Stage	35☐
Charmette	20☐
Christmas/Early Vignettes	£4–£6☐
Christmas/Middle period	£1☐
Christmas/Later issues	30☐
Chromette	20☐
Collo-Photo	30☐
Collotype	20☐
Coloured Crayon	30☐
Connoisseur/Middle period	£1☐
Connoisseur/Later issues	40☐
Continental	30☐
Continental Art	40☐
Country Life	75☐
County	60☐
Crayon	20☐
Dog Studies	75☐
Double Photo Greeting	20☐
Duo Gem	20☐
Early Tuck No. Cards	
1–10	£125 the set of 10☐
Easter/Early Vignettes	£4–£6☐
Easter/Middle period	£1☐
Easter/Later issues	30☐
Educational	£6☐
Elite	£1.50☐
Emerald Rough Sea	20☐
Emerald Sea	20☐
Empire/Early Vignettes	£10–£15☐
Fair Flowers	75☐
Floral Gems	75☐
Flower	20☐
Framed Aquagraph	30☐
Framed Charmette	20☐
Framed Gem Glosso	20☐
Framed Gem Tartan	75☐
Framed Marble	20☐
Fruit	£1.50☐
Gem	20☐
Gem Glosso	20☐
Gem Oilette	50☐
Glosso	20☐
Golden Amber Glosso	20☐
Gold Framed Gravure	20☐
Greeting/Middle period	£1☐
Greeting/Later issues	30☐
Hand Coloured Photogravure	20☐
Heraldic/Early Vignettes	£6☐
Heraldic View	£1☐
Holly	£1☐
Impressionist	£2☐
Independence Day	£3☐
Kings & Queens of England	£8☐
Landseer/Early Vignettes	£4☐
Little Hollander	£1.50☐
London	£1☐
Marine/Early Vignettes	£6☐
Monogram	£5☐
New Year/Middle period	£1☐
New Year/Later issues	30☐
North Wales	20☐
Oilette	30☐
Oilette Connoisseur	50☐

Oilette de Luxe 40☐
Olde Print 30☐
Photochrome 30☐
Photographic Pictures 50☐
Photogravure 20☐
Plate Marked 60☐
Quaint Corners 40☐
Rapholette 20☐
Rapholette Glosso 20☐
Raphotype 10☐
Realistic Roses 20☐
Real Japanese £2☐
Real Photograph 20☐
Rembrandesque 30☐
Remembrance £1☐
Rough Sea 20☐
Rural England 60☐
Rural Life £1☐
Sapphire Rough Sea 20☐
Scottish Rough Sea 20☐
Sepia 20☐
Silverette 40☐
Sporting £2☐
Sweet Sixteen £1.50☐
Thanksgiving £1.50☐
Time of Flowers 60☐
Town and City £1☐
Turneresque £1.50☐
United Kingdom £1.25☐
Valentine Posies £1.50☐
View/Early Vignettes £6☐
View/Later issues 30☐
Water Colour 20☐
Write Ahead/Early Vignettes £4.50☐
Write Away/Early Vignettes £4.50☐
Write Away/Later issues £2☐
Young Folks 50☐
Proof Editions/1000 copies £6–£8☐
Proof Editions in sets with cover (complete as issued) £40–£60☐

Re-issues – During World War 1. Some of Tuck's early postcard nos. e.g. No. 250 card, show an added verse printed on card by James B. Fagin.
Issued by Daily Telegraph £8☐

Early "Art" series – £6.

A specially commissioned Tuck card, advertising Canadian food – £8.

MISCELLANEOUS

Archaeology	15☐
Bray signed postcards	£2☐
Casinos	50–£1☐
Caves	25☐
Cameras	£1–£2☐
Clocks – Church and Town Hall	20☐
Clocks – floral	25☐
Eyes	30☐
Executions	£3+☐
Flowers	25☐
Flowers/Fruit – still life	50☐
Fruit	25☐
Friendly Societies	£1+☐
Gambling (Playing cards)	£2–£5☐
Gramophones	£2–£5☐
Inserts etc.	25☐
Jewellery	20☐
Masonic	£1.50+☐
Models	30☐
Model Making	60☐
Midgets	£1☐
Photography (good photo – unusual subject)	£1–£5☐
Photography (stereoscopic cards)	£1☐
Pottery	20☐
Opium smoking	60☐
Smoking (comic type)	75☐
Round the World Journeys	£2☐
Telephones	50–£1☐
Trees	30+☐
Trophies etc.	40☐
Torture	£2–£5☐

Must come into "Miscellaneous", but will probably need a separate listing next year – **£1.50**.

Trees – an artistic example by C.T. Howard. Cheap at 75p.

POSTAL MARKINGS ON POSTCARDS
THEIR PRICES AND/OR ADVICE ON THEIR VALUATIONS

Fig. 1
Price 25p
A common London cancellation.

GENERAL

Two books cover almost the whole field of the postal markings of the British Isles. The first is of 579 pages, copiously Illustrated but neither priced nor valuation coded, entitled *The Postmarks of Great Britain and Ireland* by R.C. Alcock and F.C. Holland published in 1940 by R.C. Alcock Ltd., of 11 Regent Street, Cheltenham. It is out of print, but like most other books may be obtained on loan through your local library or bought at Philatelic Literature Auctions from time to time at around £150. There are fifteen supplements issued to the original book which were to some extent incorporated in a small Part 2, (1954?) but this supplemental information is difficult to acquire save by those persons who have access to that superb, but alas now discontinued journal, *The Philatelic Adviser* also published by the House of Alcock. However, an abridged edition of all the foregoing entitled, *A Short History and Guide* by the same authors and publishers is now available. No one interested in the postmarks of the British Isles can really specialise, or even know for what they are looking without one or other of the above books. They are magnificent publications and may well be termed 'the bibles of British Postal Markings'. *The Philatelic Adviser Annual* for Christmas, 1963 also contained the supplements No. 1 and Nos. 9 to 15.

In early 1979, Dr J. T. Whitney produced his postmark catalogue *Collect British* Postmarks. This is a very businesslike listing of most of the postmarks mentioned in this Postmark Section of Picton's – it lists and prices, individually, most of the material the average postcard collector can expect to come across. I recommend it to all postcard collectors and dealers who want to ensure that they do not overlook the value of 'used' material that may come their way.

Now to the types themselves, but befcre dealing with each one individually the question of price(s) as shown for each needs elaboration.

GENERAL NOTES

1. Even for the period 1894 onwards, the field is vast. This catalogue covers the main types, but even within one type, its various sub-types could not possibly be dealt with in a general publication such as this. Markings from 1940 onwards are not listed.

2. Often the only sure way to discover current prices is to subscribe to the Auction Catalogues of the Philatelic Auctions which specialise in Postal History and issue *Prices Realised*. Even though Philatelic Auctions have estimated valuations inserted in their catalogues it is the price realised that matters. Many such Auctions are postal only (one cannot attend such Auctions) so that one has to wait for the list of prices realised (unfortunately these are not issued by all postal auction houses!).

3. However, for many of the types listed in this catalogue a specialist handbook exists, often fully priced or at least coded as to rarity, but with some types, no specialised price guidance exists so that many such prices are discoverable only from the sources mentioned in para. 2 and that can be a laborious task, whilst some items have not yet appeared individually at auction, but remember that Dr. J.T.Whitney's *Collect British Postmarks* now covers most of the postmarks of the British Isles from start to finish, in considerable detail - and prices them! A must for the postmark enthusiast.

Prices Scotland

Scottish Postmarks, by J.A.MacKay, MA, (1978) covers the Scottish field very thoroughly on values by a grading system.

4. This postmark section tells you:-

(a) what marking to seek,

(b) the title, author (and publisher) and date (where known) of the best specialist handbook to the compiler's knowledge and whether it contains price valuation guidance or not.

(c) representative prices of the types illustrated based on the compiler's own knowledge, dealers' lists and auction results.

5. *Prices and Condition*
These are for complete and fully readable postal markings on a presentable postcard i.e. the address side must appear pleasing for display purposes. If the marking is incomplete, or only partly readable, then the prices shown can be halved immediately save where the cancellation is particularly rare. If only vestiges of the marking remain, then downgrading must be even more drastic.

6. *A Few Technical Terms*

(a) A **Cancellation** is that part of a postal mark that obliterates the stamp so that it cannot be used again (hence, sometimes called also an 'obliteration').

(b) A **Postal Marking** covers Post Office 'additions' anywhere on a postcard and thus includes 'cancellation' (i.e. see (a) above).

(c) A **Strike** is the impression produced on a postcard by the application of an inked, hand or machine operated, piece of printing apparatus.

(d) A **Cachet** is usually a marking applied in our period other than by the Postal Authorities and not upon the adhesive stamp.

(e) **Tied**. For a postmark on cover to be considered as genuine, it must be partly on the stamp and partly on the envelope or postcard i.e. tying together the stamp and the missive upon which it has been struck. This normally proves that the stamp belongs to the particular Postcard etc. and has not been falsely attached thereto later. An untied postmark is often suspect and therefore is of less value than a tied item.

(f) **Frontally Applied**. Where the adhesive stamp is applied to the Picture side of the postcard and duly cancelled such combination is valued by philatelists at a premium because the picture often illustrates the subject of the design on the stamp and thus is most useful when exhibiting i.e. both factors are on view on the SAME side.

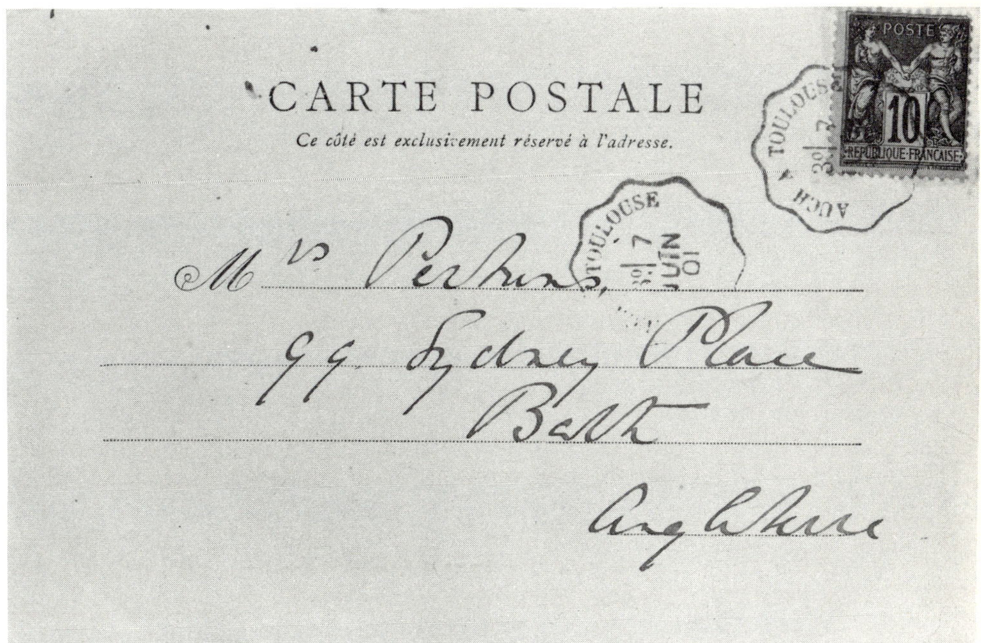

French 'wavy circle' Travelling Rail Post Office Auch to Toulouse - Price £3.

DUPLEX

This is fig. 1(a) and consists of a c.d.s. (this means circular date stamp) containing the name of the sender's post office, date and time of cancellation plus a barred canceller with a number in the centre. There are different types for England (and Wales), Scotland and Ireland and most of the more important Post Offices had their own particular number. A book entitled *British Post Office Numbers 1844-1906* by G.Brumell and recently re-printed by R.C. Alcock & Son Ltd. of 11, Regent Street, Cheltenham covers the whole range (it also contains about 70 pages of illustrated text on postmarks). The 'Duplex' is really a cancellation of the Victorian era, but it survived in smaller Post Offices well into the 20th century.

Fig. 1 (a)

The price of cards bearing this marking is from 25p to £25 or more depending on the size of the population served by the Post Office concerned or the number of years it was in use. Obviously the less the number of examples surviving, the higher the price.

Note: In 1975 R.G. Trail and F.C. Holland produced their book *The Sideways Duplex Cancellations of England and Wales* (published by R.C. Alcock of Cheltenham) with a rarity guide which has increased the popularity of this postmark tremendously, i.e. where the name of the Post Office is *sideways on* to the numeral section (price £1 upwards).

The compiler of the Postmark sections of this catalogue has produced a provisional price guide to all the numbers allocated to post offices in England and Wales from 1844 through Edwardian Days to the early George V period. Each number is rarity graded to a price. See the advertisment in this catalogue for this book. Occasionally the c.d.s. part of the duplex is absent, the cancellation being solely performed by the numeral cancellation.

SQUARED CIRCLE

A book entitled *Squared Circle Postmarks* by W.G. Stitt-Dibden dated 1964 and printed and published by the British Postmark Society lists in 28 pages with illustrations, all the known usages (unpriced). It also traces the evolution of the postmark from the experimental types of later Victorian times, which are also illustrated, to its more general form, fig. 2. An early variety is fig. 3. below.

Fig. 2.
Price 50p to £2 or more
(i.e. more for the 'smaller' Post Offices).

Fig. 3.
Price (Scarce) £5.

SINGLE CIRCLE C.D.S.

Fig. 4 shows a characteristic single circle date stamp canceller. You will note that it is larger than fig. 5 which, because of its smaller diameter is called a 'thimble' and these latter seem quite popular.

Fig. 4
Price 25p to £1

Fig. 5
Price £1 to £3
(but it must be of small diameter).

DOUBLE CIRCLE C.D.S.

Fig. 6 is a typical English example with post town, two arcs and a code at base inside two concentric rings with date and time in the centre space. It is the commonest of all 20th century cancellations.

Fig. 6
Price 10p

THE SCROLL (SOMETIMES CALLED 'HOODED CIRCLE' OR 'CRESTED CIRCLE').

The 'Scroll' Fig. 7 is really a single circle c.d.s. but with the post office name inscribed in a scroll surrounding and external to the top half of the circular postmark. Usually used in London and the price shown is for that area. If used in Liverpool or certain Irish towns, prices can be doubled or trebled and there are rarities like Waterford (£20).

Fig. 7
Price £3

HOSTER, PART OF

Fig. 8 may be considered as being just a single circle c.d.s. with a duplication of the outer rim. It is however, thought to be adapted from a larger post mark used in Victorian times called "The Hoster" (which is a valuable postmark of that period).

Fig. 8
Price £4

THE HAMMER

Fig. 9 has been nicknamed 'the hammer' as apparently the handstamp was applied in hammer fashion. It originated on the continent and is common in Germany (and Switzerland) thus accounting for another name applied to it,"The German type". It is very scarce and a clear strike infrequent. Its characteristics are the full date and time between the two lines across the centre of the stamp with the small semi-circle above and below with vertical line-shading therein.

Fig. 9
Price £50 (rare)

Fig. 10
Price £3 to £10
Becoming very much sought after.
Price depends upon clarity of strike and size of locality.

SKELETONS (Fig. 10.)

These are rather scarce because they fulfilled transient needs, e.g.

1) to replace, in emergency, handstamps lost or damaged at any permanent Post Office, or,

2) to be used temporarily, say at some special event, where a mobile Post Office was set up for a short period and for this reason it is sometimes called "a travelling stamp".

It varies from a very large circle to a comparatively small one. Generally those found are large single circles with the usual data therein, but not symmetrically arranged, as it was assembled by hand with moveable 'type' so the test is, are the names and dating items balancing? If not, it is most likely to be a Skeleton whatever its diameter. Often the strike is very poor. (Handbook *The Skeleton Postmarks of Great Britain* by George F. Crabb, 1960, published by the British Postmark Society. No valuation data but it covers the subject most exhaustively). Many Irish postmarks appear to be 'skeletons' but the data 'balances' so that they are the normal type (see Fig 4) of single c.d.s. and are not skeletons.

Fig. 11 shows a single machine postal marking consisting of a large c.d.s. with a seven line canceller containing within the lines 'E ♔ R' which means (E)dward (R)ex. There is a similar postal mark for Queen Victoria 'V ♔ R'.

Fig. 11.

Price £1.50
Price for the earlier VR type £4

MACHINE CANCELLATIONS

For the specialist this is one of the most complicated postmark fields of the turn of the century. The Post Office was trying to speed up cancelling by using machinery instead of handstamps. Many machines were tried. Some are common, some are very rare and the variety of strikes runs into hundreds. It is impossible to try and depict them all here. A few examples are shown but reference should be made to the following handbooks:-

(a) *The Hey-Dolphin Machines of Great Britain* by W.G. Stitt-Dibden & J.W.A. Lowden, published by the authors in 1959. (No valuation data). Illustrated.

(b) *Columbia Stamp Cancelling Machines at the E.C.D.O. 1901-7* by Jason T.W. Mann Ph.D., D.I.C., by the Postal History Society, 1963. (No valuation data). Illustrated.

(c) *Early Stamp Machines* by W.G. Stitt-Dibden, published by the Postal History Society, 1964. (No valuation data). Illustrated.

LONDON.E.
3 15 —PM No.18.
DEC20'05

Fig. 12

This is a typical straight (six) line canceller with P.O., date and time inserted in gaps in the lines

Normally, Price 10p but the No. of the machine used '18' is shown in this example and thus this particular strike is valued at 50p.

Fig. 13
Price 15p
A typical wavy (five) line canceller with single circle c.d.s.

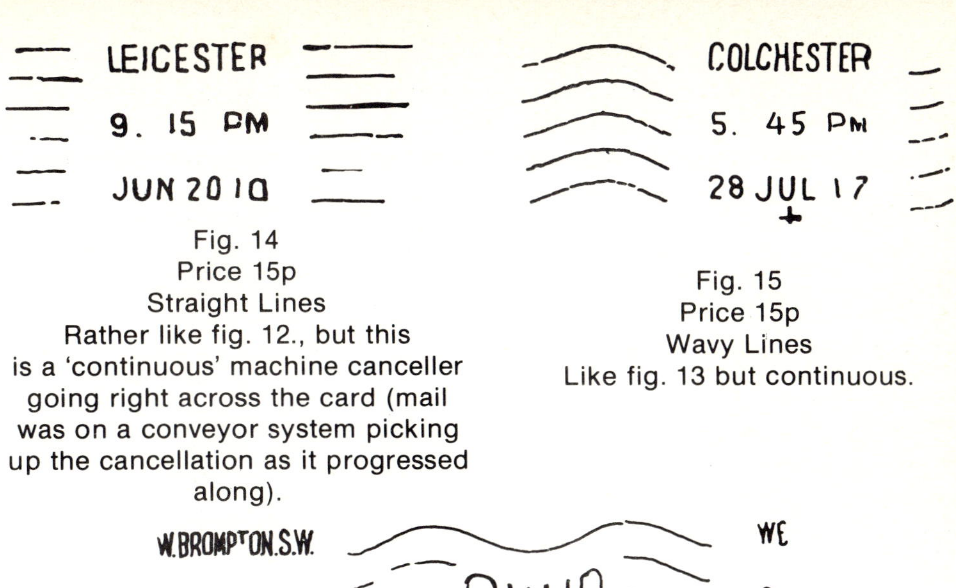

Fig. 14
Price 15p
Straight Lines
Rather like fig. 12., but this is a 'continuous' machine canceller going right across the card (mail was on a conveyor system picking up the cancellation as it progressed along).

Fig. 15
Price 15p
Wavy Lines
Like fig. 13 but continuous.

Fig. 16

Fig. 16 above is like the continuous fig. 15, but note the large S.W.10 inserted in the wavy lines.
Price £6

Many varieties pricing up to £10 exist in the machine cancellation field. Any marking in the 'lines' aimed at the identification of the user or place of usage of a canceller always warrants a premium.

SLOGANS

These started in 1917 with "BUY NATIONAL WAR BONDS NOW" and over 100 different types appeared before the end of 1939 (after that date especially after W.W.2., the numbers issued each year rose steeply).

BUY NATIONAL WAR BONDS NOW
(Continuous)
Fig. 17
Price 25p

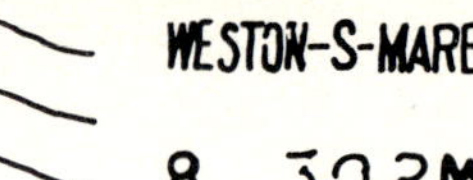

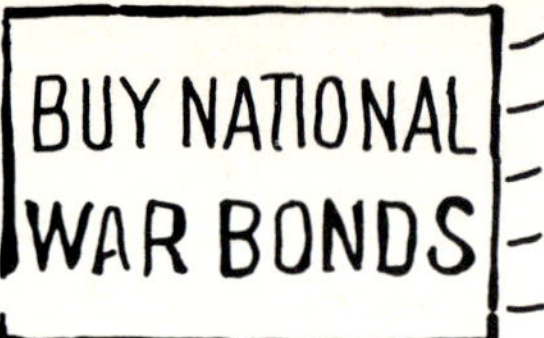

Fig. 18.

BUY NATIONAL WAR BONDS (WITHOUT 'NOW')
(Continuous)

Price 30p

THE TELEPHONE
A SOUND INVESTMENT

Fig. 18a

THE TELEPHONE A SOUND INVESTMENT

Price 75p

OXFORD
11. 45 AM
21 OCT 18

FEED THE GUNS
WITH WAR BONDS

Fig. 19

FEED THE GUNS WITH WAR BONDS
Price 50p

BRITISH GOODS
ARE BEST

Fig. 20.

BRITISH GOODS ARE BEST
Price 15p

Fortunately a superb handbook *Slogan Postmarks of the United Kingdom* by Cyril R.H. Parsons and George R. Pearson, published in July 1965 exists showing every slogan, illustrated (where necessary) and priced. The interest in slogans seems weak owing to the fact that new ones in recent times are appearing in great quantity every year but those to 1939 are getting scarce. At the moment, the prices in the handbook mentioned have not, in my opinion, increased very much, proof that demand really controls prices. Yearly supplements have been issued to this Handbook to keep it right up to date.

Fig. 20a
EMPLOYMENT SLOGAN

Price £1

THE WILKINSON EXPERIMENT

Keep your weather eye open for this postal marking. It is unique (fig. 21). It looks like a common mark applied to bulk circulars as the word 'paid' appears, but it has also 'postage' before the word 'paid'. It was used between the 25th January 1912 and the end of August 1912. This marking was produced by a system whereby one placed, a postcard for example, into a machine which could be operated for 1d that made the impression fig. 21 in lieu of your using an adhesive stamp. The postcard could then be placed in the letter box for normal delivery as it was 'postage paid'. Only one machine was installed, in London, and the impression made was in red. It was also postmarked later like any other correspondence, but in red to show that its cost of transport had already been paid (its usage dispensed with adhesive stamps).

Fig. 21

Price £35 on Postcard (but see below).

If dated 25th January 1912 only £25 as the usual philatelic first day enthusiasm for this machine occured but its use dropped sharply after the first day. (The last day, 31st August 1912 is also worth less for the same reason). Its use was abandoned on the grounds of mechanical break-down and low security. See a fuller account by W.G. Stitt-Dibden in his *Early Stamp Machines.*

METER MARKS

These were used in Great Britain from 1922 (May 13th) and occur at times on postcards carrying personal messages, although they were normally meant for business usage. They are not often seen, and should be treated as 'gimmicks' on postcards.

Fig. 22

Price 30p

Handbook – *Meter Stamps of Great Britain and Ireland* (Eire) by J.C. Mann. 2nd Edition 1972. Fully priced.

MB - MOBILE BOX (OR IN FRENCH BOITE MOBILE - BM)

Vessels plying between France and England carried a portable "locked" letter box located near the gangplank, in which, in either country, mail could be posted so availing itself of the immediate transport service thus provided. On its arrival say from France at a British Port, the box was handed to the local Post Office for opening and its contents cancelled MB (meaning Mobile Box) to indicate its source (the French arrival ports used BM). They are quite scarce and listed in full in the *Maritime Postal History of the British Isles* by Alan Robertson, circa 1958 (the valuation guide to that work is a separate 24 page booklet which also evaluates almost all the known British Maritime 'Markings').

Fig. 23
Price minimum £6 on Card (50p on piece).
(Other ports to £50)

Fig. 23a
LONDON M.B.
Price minimum £6

TRIANGLES

These triangular obliterations with apex upwards when reading the letters began in 1895 to be used in connection with the bulk cancelling of 'Imitation' typewritten circulars (at a lower postal rate). Originally they were single handstamps. At the beginning of the reign of Edward VII machine cancelling was introduced and the c.d.s. usually found in such cancellations was sometimes replaced by a triangle.

These letters consisted of the telegraph office code of the Post Office concerned. They were replaced later by the Post Office number of the place in question.

Fig. 24
Price 50p to £1

POSTAGE DUE AND OTHER POSTAL EXPLANATORY MARKINGS

A book entitled *A Catalogue of Great Britain Surcharge and Explanatory Dies* by Colin M. Langston (circa 1960) covers the subject very well indeed. It is illustrated, but with no price indications. This subject is not that philatelically popular so that the great bulk of the material values between 25p and £1 and more usually towards the lower figure, but there are rarities. Those with Postage Due adhesive stamps applied bring them to the higher end of the price scale. There are upwards of 500 different kinds of explanatory markings.

Fig. 25
Price 25p to £1

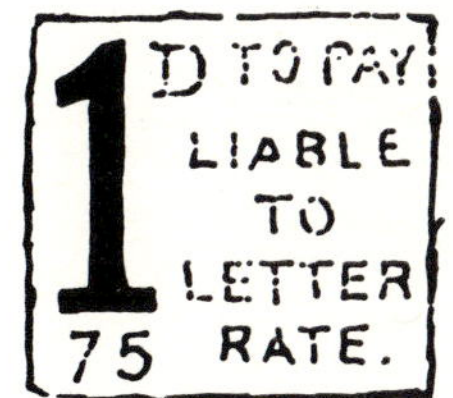

Fig. 26
Price 25p to £1

N.B. The numeral or alpha-numeral beneath the 'tax' charge can refer to a scarce small post office when it will attract a substantial premium. Estimate about half the valuation shown in the book *Numeral Cancellations of England and Wales* (1979) by M.R.Hewlett.

MISSORTS

Those with the apex of a *small* triangle pointing **downwards** when reading the 'Code', were used to indicate that a postcard had been wrongly allocated within the Railway sorting system – one of the National Railway Divisions i.e. N.W. equals North West. There are half a dozen 'compass' or similar designations for the Railway sub-divisions of the country.

Fig. 27
Price 50p to £1

RAILWAY MARKINGS

With a **Station** name in the postmark (usually a c.d.s., see fig. 28) the price varies from 50p to £5 depending upon the importance of the station, i.e. the less well known and/or less frequently used, the higher the value.

Fig. 28
Price 50p to £5

Fig. 29
Price 50p to £3

With **R.S.O.** (meaning Railway Sub-Office) in the c.d.s. it indicates a post office which receives its mail from a T.P.O. The Post Office can be on, near or far from, a railway line.

Fig. 29a

A Single Ring
R.S.O. from Scotland
Price £3

Travelling Post Offices (T.P.O's) or **Travelling Sorting Carriages.** These previous types are relatively common but the markings indicating that postcards were cancelled in a Sorting Carriage whilst the train was moving are scarce and much prized.
The markings are by no means standard.

Fig. 30

This shows the two towns between which the train travelled whilst it carried mail being sorted in transit. (S.C. is the abbreviation for Sorting Carriage).

Price £8

Fig. 31.

This shows the two towns and T.P.O. (Travelling Post Office) and Down (Direction).

Price £10

Fig. 32.

This shows a Sorting Carriage. (Quite Common)
Price £2.50

Fig. 33

This shows the name of the Railway Company, T.P.O. and the direction of travel of the train i.e. going East.

Price £3

There is no specialist handbook showing valuation codes or prices T.P.O's. Actual experience of sale prices alone can tell you, but within the 1894–1939 period those up to 1919 price between £2.50 and £15 depending upon the degree of importance of the route and how early was the usage - the less the usage and the earlier its date, the higher its value. After 1919 and up to 1939, £2 to £4 is probably nearer the mark, but, there are exceptions and some obscure T.P.O.'s may be found throughout this later period worth up to the £10 mark. There are a few fine handbooks (without valuations) to guide you in your searches and they give the period of use. Normally, if the "strike" obliterates the stamp it is worth more than a strike applied elsewhere on the card.

T.P.O. HANDBOOKS

(a) *Irish T.P.O.'s* by C.W. Ward 1938 (no valuations).

(b) *Scottish T.P.O.'s* by C.W. Ward 1947 (no valuations).

(c) *English T.P.O.'s* by C.W. Ward 1948 which includes Welsh T.P.O.'s (no valuations).

(d) *T.P.O., Part 1 The Specials and Associated T.P.O.'s* by H.S. Wilson 1971. Well illustrated. (no valuations).

(e) *T.P.O. Part 2 England - South of the Midland T.P.O.* by H.S. Wilson 1975 (no valuations)

(f) *The Railway Travelling Post Offices of Great Britain and Ireland 1838–1975* by Norman Hill 1977 (no valuations).

AIR POST

Fortunately for the Philatelic Specialist in Aviation, Messrs. Francis J. Field of Sutton Coldfield published the following book *50 years of British Air Mails 1911–1960* compiled by N.C. Baldwin and reprinted in 1968 which will suffice for most purposes (the same firm have published many other useful specialist books on Air mails). The handbook quoted is fully priced and illustrated. One of our earliest official aeroplane flights in Great Britain is shown here.

Fig. 34. see over for caption

London to Windsor flown postcard dated September 9th, 1911. Price from £15 flown, but the price depends upon the colour of the picture and whether the flight originated in Windsor or London. (From Windsor to London the prices are double i.e. £30).

Special Handbook. *The Coronation Aerial Post, 1911* by Field, F.J. and Baldwin, N.C., 1934 (includes valuation).
Aerophilatelic price realisations in CMA Auctions 1973/75 from CMA Auctions P.O. Box 20 Bergvliet, 7864, South Africa (covers World flights).

Fig. 35
Price £5

This obliteration should rightly come under Exhibitions, but it is included here for convenience of subject, i.e. the 1934 Air Post Exhibition.

SEA POST

PAQUEBOT (OR 'SHIP LETTER' OR OTHER NATIONAL LANGUAGE EQUIVALENT).

When a seagoing vessel has cards written by its crew or passengers, on board, they usually stamp such correspondence with the adhesives of the country to which the ship belongs and/or by which it is operated. On reaching a port in a foreign country, the mail is taken ashore to the Local Post Office and in order to "explain" the foreign stamps on the cards and to facilitate their onward transmission the word 'paquebot' or its equivalent is applied (sometimes as a canceller of the adhesive or sometimes as an adjoining extra postal mark). Paquebot means literally 'packet boat'. Two books cover the subject magnificently in all respects.

(a) *Paquebots Cancellations of the World* by Roger Hosking M.A. 1977. This is the latest definitive work and gives 6 rarity grades to help evaluation (190 pages fully illustrated). I suggest you treat grades AA to A as under £2 value and D as £10 plus but these are for the year 1980 remember.

(b) For a superb highly specialised monumental work on all British Maritime Markings (and I mean all) I refer you to *The Maritime Postal Markings of the British Isles* by the late Alan Robertson. This consists of five sections lettered A to E, in special holders plus a most valuable priced guide dated 1958.

Section E is the most vital part and when allied with the separate Valuation Guide it enables you to recognise any mark quickly and accurately with its **1958 price.** There is also a separate index (and a bibliography).

Fig. 36
A typical **additional** Paquebot marking

Price £1 (Landed at Port Said).
Price of others to £15

Fig. 37
Paquebot applied as an obliteration (of the stamp)

Price £3
(Landed at Plymouth)

Prices of other British Sea Ports and other Countries to £15

Fig. 38
A c.d.s. type Paquebot

Price £2.50
(Landed at Bombay).

A Ship's cachet showing the source from which mail has emanated.
Price £2.50
(To be added to the value of the Paquebot marking used). If this cachet contains the name of the ship concerned then the price can vary from £3 to £20.

Fig. 39

BRISTOL
SHIP-LETTER

Fig. 40

A 'Ship Letter' example

Price £40

(i.e. Landed at Bristol).

Fig. 41

Sea Post Office. A Travelling Post Office Mark' on the Aden-India run in our period.

Price 75p (common)

COASTAL TRAFFIC - BRITISH ISLES.

Fig. 42
Clyde Steamers
Greenock-Ardrishaig
Packet.

S.S. Columba £25
S.S. Iona £35
S.S. Grenadier £120
S.S. Chevalier £200

POSTED ON
"LA MARGUERITE"

Fig. 43
North Wales Steamers
The private cachet of the 'La Marguerite', a pleasure steamer plying between Liverpool, Llandudno, Beaumaris and/or Menai Bridge.

Price £18 (Straight Line) - £40 (Circular)
S.S. St. Tudno £250 (Circular)
S.S. Snowdon £300 (Circular)

NAVAL SECURITY - DUMB CANCELS

Naval Security Markings (used during hostilities to avoid indicating where Naval vessels docked or were stationed).

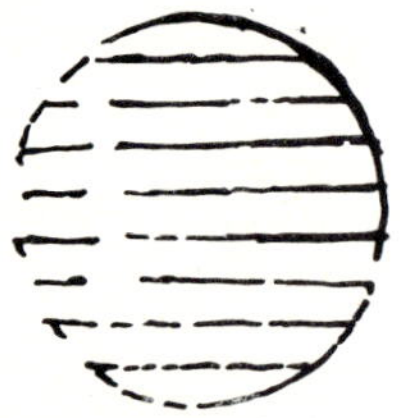

Fig. 44
Dumb Cancels applied on mail from Naval vessels etc. to comply with shipping security.
Prices £1 to £8 depending upon the rarity and shape of the canceller.

Fig. 45
F.P.O.a. is the one Naval type that is similar to those used by the Army Field Post Offices.
Used to maintain anonymity.

Price £3

RECEIVED FROM H.M.SHIP
NO CHARGE TO BE RAISED

Fig. 46 (and similar)
Price 75p

Mail from Naval Personnel.

Fig. 47

A Cachet
Price £20
A rare hybrid of 1918 for the Naval Air Service

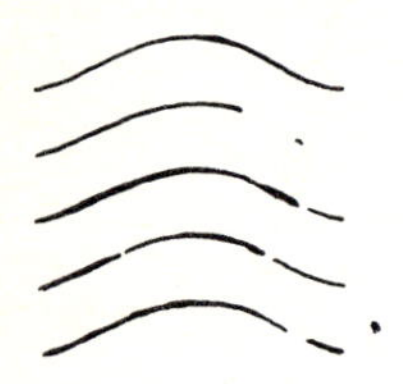
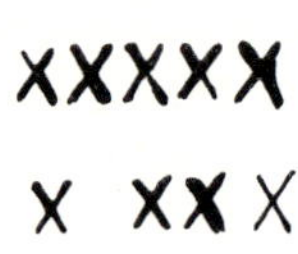
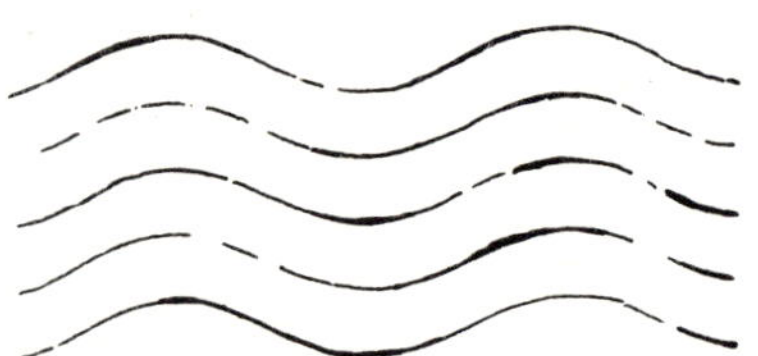
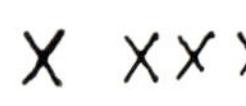

Fig. 47(a)
Price £4
Another Naval Dumb Cancel - Machine

MILITARY MARKS

CAMPS

See *Camp Postmarks of the United Kingdom* by R.A. Kingston, 1971 (and the 1974 supplement) published by the Forces Postal History Society. No valuations.

Such markings may vary in value from 50p to £10 depending upon the date upon which the Camp was set up, its duration and the type of canceller used.

Fig. 48

Duplex of Strensall Camp

Price £6

Fig. 49

Double circle c.d.s. (Bowood Camp)

Price £4

MILITARY - WORLD WAR 1 SECURITY NUMBERS AND/OR LETTERS USED IN LIEU OF PLACE NAMES

Fig. 50

Army Post Office
(No. S.X.2 was used in Salonica, Greece).

Price £4

HANDBOOKS

(a) A hand book *The Postal History of the British Army in World War 1* (before and after) 1903-1929 by Alistair Kennedy and George Crabb (1977) lists and prices as at 1977 all the known markings (and allocates them too!) A superb philatelic production. (N.B. 'Pictons' gives in its 1977 Postcard Catalogue some generalised valuation guidance).

(b) *The Post and Censor and other Marks 1914-1919 from Prisoners of War letters* by F.J. Carter (1939). No valuations. Covers most belligerents.

OTHER MARKINGS OF W.W.1.

Examples from World War 1

British P.O.W.s in Turkey to £50

Internees in the Isle of Man to £75

British Empire forces of World War 1 are also another quite different subject, e.g. the Indian Troops which served in many military theatres have provided valuable security markings. (£2 to £25).

GENERAL NOTE ON MILITARY P.O. NUMBERS

In all these markings, if the code number of the post office is not readable in full, it loses most of its value as a postal item because it is not possible, normally, to allocate the card to its area of usage. Censor marks on these and other postcards are not, philatelically speaking, valued very highly, except where they give clues to the location of an otherwise indecipherable military post office 'code'. In general censor marks hardly warrant a premium unless there is something unusual about them.

THE BOER WAR - SOUTH AFRICAN WAR 1899-1902.

A most popular subject. Many stamps of Great Britain were used and postmarked in the war area in South Africa and these are valued in Messrs Stanley Gibbon's British Commonwealth Catalogue.

Full details without valuation are to be found of the P.OW. camp marks in two fine handbooks produced by the Anglo-Boer War Philatelic Society.

Part A *Philately of the Boer and British P.O.W. Camps in South Africa and the Burgher Camps.*

Part B *P.O.W. Camps Overseas*

Both of these books are main-titled *The Anglo-Boer War (1899-1902)*

PHILATELIC CONGRESSES

These are all listed and priced in the handbook *Special Event Postmarks of the United Kingdom* by George R. Pearson (May 1963). This deals with the subject exhaustively and is a 'must' for any G.B. Postmark collector.

Fig. 52
Price £10
This was the first Congress (1909)

Fig. 53
Price £5
(1929 Congress)

EXHIBITIONS

This subject is covered by the handbook referred to above and in addition is dealt with in a slightly more specialised form in a handbook entitled *A Priced Catalogue of British Exhibitions 1840–1940.* by W. G. Stitt-Dibden, published by the Argyle Stamp Co. Ltd. 1962. It was a good guide to prices in 1962 but inflation has now rendered it out of date in that respect.

Fig. 54
Price £10

Fig. 55
Price £2 (Common)

WEMBLEY EXHIBITION
1924–1925

This exhibition had a feast of postal markings, partly listed in the two handbooks already mentioned under the Exhibitions section but also covered in a specialised, but unpriced form by W.G. Stitt-Dibden in Vol. 1 *Wembley and Olympic Issues*, published jointly by two of our foremost Philatelic Societies specialising in the postal markings of Great Britain, namely 'The Postal History Society' and 'The Great Britain Philatelic Society'. Many Wembley 'Markings' also rank as slogans so that the handbook mentioned under slogans also refers to this section.

Fig. 56
A Common slogan
Price 50p

CHRISTMAS DAY

(A special Mark to delay delivery till the 25th December)

This subject is covered by *Posted in Advance for Delivery on Christmas Day* by Cyril Kidd, published by Robson Lowe Ltd., 50, Pall Mall, London SW1Y 5JZ dated 1974. He grades all known markings used for this special purpose from 'A – low' to 'D – extremely rare'. They were used between 1902 and 1909 mainly in the counties of Lancashire, Cheshire and Yorkshire, but also in a few other English town as well as Douglas in the Isle of Man and a few places in Scotland and Ireland. Some ten different types were used. Its object was to mark mail that was posted *before* Christmas Day in such a manner that the receiving Post Office would hold it back for delivery on Christmas Day itself. All are very scarce except those of Liverpool and Manchester which value between £50 and £100 for the commoner types.

Fig. 57

Price on Postcard £100 to £300

Fig. 58

Price on Postcard £100 to £300
S.C.R. is the telegraphic code for Sale in Cheshire

(A Full Mark on Piece 1/5th of above prices. On loose stamp - part strike - 1/10th). See *Stamp Collecting* for 2nd December 1976 for a complete price listing of all towns and years by the compiler of this section of this catalogue.

ISLAND POSTMARKS

This is a vast subject which has a strong fascination for specialist postmark collectors. The Channel Islands, Lundy Island and the Isle of Man are particularly popular.

Any stamp on a postcard bearing a cancellation containing the name of an Island Post Office is worth a premium. The smaller the Island having such a Post Office, the higher the premium and similarly small Sub-Post Offices on the larger Islands are much prized. Some handbooks exist as under:-

1. *Priced Catalogue of Channel Island Postal Markings* by O.W. Newport. This is a fine illustrated handbook. (Mr. Newport has also written later handbooks dealing more deeply with the more recent issues). Annually revised editions.

2. *Collect Channel Island Stamps* - Published by Stanley Gibbons (Annually revised editions).

3. *Isle of Man Catalogue of Stamps and Postal History* - 1979 edition compiled by Dr. J.T.Whitney.

4. *Collect Isle of Man Stamps* - Published by Stanley Gibbons.

5. *Handbook and Catalogue of the Stamps and Postmarks of the Islands of Great Britain* by Woodcote (Stamps) of Surrey is the best source embracing valuation I know - date *circa* 1961. It dealt with every island, however small that ever had its own Post Office. The publication is a rare item to find these days.

GENERAL PRICES

From say 25p for a common Isle of Wight Post Office to £35 for a Lundy Island Postmark (not on a 'local' Lundy Island Stamp but on one of the Great Britain issues). Jersey and Guernsey from £2 to £10 or more for a small Sub-Post Office of either Island. Alderney £12.

Fig. 59
Price £9 Sark.

Fig. 60
Price £4 (Gorey - Jersey)

Fig. 60(b)
St. Kilda
Price £25

Fig. 60(a)
Lundy Island
Price £35

ABERRATIONS (or RUBBERS)

Sometimes in small Post Offices cancellers that were meant for telegram forms or parcels or some internal usage were incorrectly or accidentally or in emergency, brought into use for cancelling the stamps on postcards. They are almost always single c.d.s. strikes and in colour range from mauve to 'blues' verging on black.

Fig. 61
Normal Rubber
If clear £5
Only £1 if
partly indistinct

Fig. 62
Temporary three or four
Line Rubber
If clear £8 (scarce)
Only £2 if
partly indistinct

ROYAL HOUSEHOLDS

These obviously are scarce and include cards **addressed to** Royal Personages. This is a highly specialised field with prices always in the pounds and even those *sent* to Royalty are worth a good few pence. (For further information refer *Alcock & Holland, Postmarks of Great Britain and Ireland*, Section P, pages 587–588) Auction Sales will also give you valuation data but specific pricing is impossible as each item has to be treated on its merits.

'ANACHRONISMS' (i.e. Used out of chronological order)

In an emergency to obliterate a stamp that has missed the ordinary cancelling procedure, one finds obsolete handstamps being used to deface such items. Sometimes in connection with some internal postal checking or census procedure, an old '1844' canceller is taken into use.

Fig. 63
Price £10
(An '1844' handstamp).
Not a Duplex

CORK CANCELS

Fig. 64
Price £2 to £5

CORK CANCELS

These were used by Naval security and also by the Post Office where ordinary mail 'missed cancellation" at its place of origination, i.e. the place of arrival someties killed or cancelled the 'unused' stamp anonymously by using a 'dumb' or cork cancel.

FIRST DAY COVERS

See the Special Section now devoted to this subject (refer to Table of Contents).

These dated items are highly prized nowadays and worth seeking. They add enormously to the value of otherwise common postmarks.

CACHETS

These are markings applied usually other than by the *Official* Post Office Services. They may be classed as 'gimmicks' but they are nevertheless of value.

Fig. 65 and similar
Price 50p to £2
Lands End

Fig. 66
Price £1 to £2.50
Summit of Snowdon

COUNTRY INTERCHANGES

Often one finds a stamp of Great Britain cancelled by the postmark of another Country and vice versa. Usually this occurs in connection with Paquebot Usage where it is in association with a 'sea' marking. One can usually infer that a 'Paquebot' marking should have been applied, but that instead, the card has received only the local, port name, canceller. These always intrigue Postmark Collectors and Rank for a premium of £1 upwards.

Readers should note that Ascension Island, a British Island Colony in the South Atlantic used the stamps of Great Britain until 1922 with the cancellation 'Ascension', usually rather faint, but if readable it is a valuable postmark. (See *Stanley Gibbons British Commonwealth Catalogue* for extensive valuation data - £25 a card is a quite common auction realisation).

OUR RAREST CANCELLATION

In the period 1894-1939 which this Postal Section covers, the 1898 'Flag Cancel' which was used on four days only, in 1898, and possibly to cancel less than 7,000 pieces of correspondence, is considered by your compiler to be our rarest cancellation, as only two copies have been mentioned in the Philatelic Press, but one or two more have been reported to the compiler as being known to exist, but they have not been seen by him.

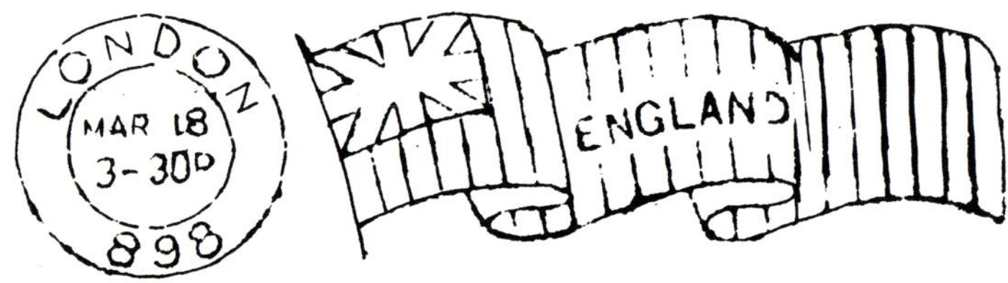

Fig. 67

Price. I would estimate at Auction these days £400. (See the special article in the *Stamp Magazine* for June, 1971 by the compiler of this catalogue).

'PERFINS'

(Value as a gimmick from £1, on postcard of course)

I shall offend my 'perfin' friends if I do not refer to this aspect sometimes found incorporated in the adhesive stamps appearing on postcards. To prevent the stealing of stamps and their subsequent resale or private use, many firms had small holes made in their stamps either depicting the initials (or full name) of their firms or some motif. This is called a 'Perfin'. We will not comment therefore on their use on postcards, but such pierced stamps do appear on private pictorial postcards! If you want to know more about this fascinating aspect of philately, there are the following handbooks:-

(a) *The Handbook of British Perfins* by John S. Nelson – 1967 (no valuations).

(b) *Catalogue of G.B. Official Perfins* by the Great Britain Philatelic Society, compiled by Mary E. Thornton (1967) with a rarity guide.

MISCELLANEOUS

Ocean T.P.O.'s

Fig. 68
A rare maritime T.P.O.
(U.K. to S.A.)
Price £30

Edinburgh Cuts

Fig. 69
A special Edinburgh
'Broken' Arc code
Price £10

MISSORT

Fig. 70
A London Missort c.d.s.
Price £4 (scarce)

CACHET

Fig. 71
Cruise of 'Northern Belle'
Price £30

A POSTMARK THAT HAS BEEN OVERLOOKED

The Sub-Office c.d.s.

(c.d.s. means circular date stamp)

The address side of the postcard shown here (Fig. 72) indicates that it has been posted, apparently at Winslow, Bucks, and the stamp has been cancelled with that name and with 894 in the obliterator. However, you will notice also on the card, a single circle date stamp (and name-place) for North Marston, 3 miles from Winslow. This is the sub-office where the postcard was originally posted but the post office in that village (it usually indicates a village or a town suburb) did NOT sort its mail but just collected it and sent it into its HEAD office for sorting and merely applied its local stamp to show its Head Office from whence the missive had originated.

These are small places as a rule and Local Postal Historians are seeking these markings now – in fact it is not known preceisely how many villages did apply their 'sub-post office stamps' so that some rarities are going to exist. Many of these are 'thimble' size which gives another bonus to the mark. I tentatively price these larger sub-office postmarks at a minimum £1 and the smaller villages and the hamlets up to £5 at least. When the penny drops, I foresee a scramble for them by the Local Postal Historians. Remember these marking do **not** cancel the stamp, the Head Office does that cancelling with its c.d.s. and/or obliterator. Do not confuse this despatch sub-office c.d.s. with that of the point of delivery c.d.s. to the addressee, which is more generally in use and thus attracts no real premium at present.

SUB-POST OFFICE C.D.S.
(not used as a canceller)

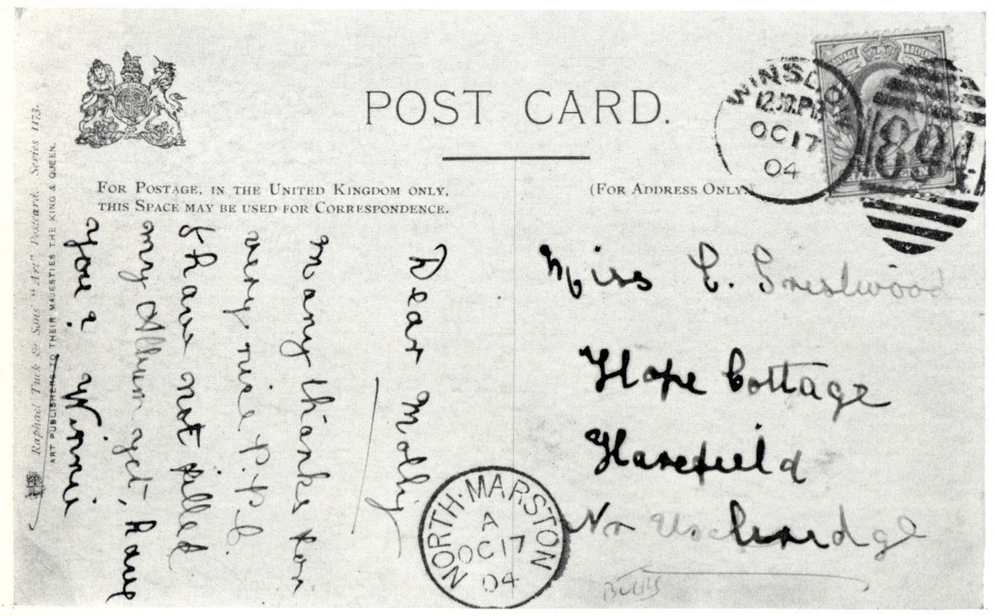

Fig. 72
est. £5 (soon)

ANOTHER OVERLOOKED POSTMARK
The Scottish double ring c.d.s.
(c.d.s. means circular date stamp)

Fig. 73 shows a typical Scottish double ring c.d.s. carrying a number in the double ring at the bottom (382). This is the local post office number. Except for a few places in England to be mentioned later, only Scotland used this local post office number in this way. It must NOT be confused with the low numbers found for places in England, Wales and Scotland which denoted NOT the number of the Post Office but the number of the cancelling handstamp held at the Office which is a comparatively unimportant fact.

There are over 700 such different numbers for Scotland. I would suggest a price of 50p for the larger town and £5 or more for some of the tiny villages.

Birmingham (75) Liverpool (466) Haswell (K34) Murton Colliery (K35) South Hetton (K36) and possibly Manchester (498) all in England also used this Scottish type c.d.s. There will be no premium for the three large towns but postcards carrying a good, well-aligned postmark of K34, K45 or K36 will be worth at least £5 each.

To avoid mistaking the handstamp reference number for a 'place' numeral cancellation, check such numbers against the early lists of offices and numbers issued by the Post Office and reproduced in Brumell. (Only numbers under 60 need real checking).

SCOTTISH DOUBLE RING C.D.S.

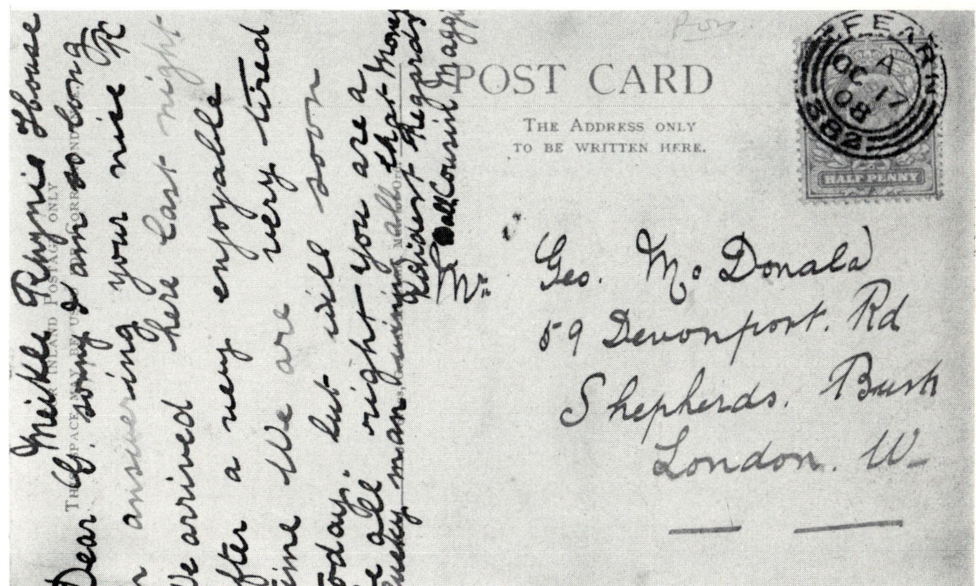

Fig. 73 est. £4

CONCLUSION

These sections on postmarks should alert all postcard owners to the need for them to examine their postally used material more closely. By now readers will have appreciated the magnitude of the task of trying to cover this enormous field in a few pages, but for most types the compiler has shown where to find the specialist information or where none exists he has advised on how to make some realistic self assessment.

N.B. Most of the specialist books mentioned in this section and elsewhere in this catalogue can be obtained from our Literature advertisers but if those sources fail you, then ask your local lending library to try and get them through their exchange service if it is not held locally (the fee for this service is very small).

Bermuda – Block of four with Hamilton cancellation – Price £4.

FIRST DAY POSTCARDS
(BEARING ADHESIVE STAMPS)

In Philatelic circles a postcard bearing an adhesive stamp cancelled with a date stamp showing the first day of the issue of such stamp often carries a very large premium over the price of the same stamp used later.

EXAMPLES	**Est. Value**
VICTORIAN G.B.	
½d Blue Green dated 17 April, 1900 (its value later is not even one penny!)	£250
EDWARDIAN	
½d Blue Green dated 1 January, 1902 (De La Rue)	£50
1d Red dated 1 January, 1902 (De La Rue)	£50
GEORGIAN (FIRST DAY DATES)	
½d Green (three-quarter face Downey Head) dated 22 June, 1911	£50
1d Red (three-quarter face Downey Head over crouching lion) also dated 22nd June, 1911	£65
WEMBLEY 1924 23rd April Special Exhibition Stamp 1d	£50
WEMBLEY 1924 23rd April Special Exhibition Stamp 1½d	£75
WEMBLEY 1925 9th May Special Exhibition Stamp 1d	£120
WEMBLEY 1925 9th May Special Exhibition Stamp 1½d	£250

There are many other First Day dates not shown here but they have all been dealt with most efficiently by Messrs. B.H.Townsend and A.Buckingham in their book *First Day Covers* obtainable from Bredon Hill Stamps, P.O. Box 12, Evesham, Worcs, or Benham, 53A, High Street, Hythe, Kent (Annual revised editions).

Stamps above the 1½d value are not often found on postcards before 1940 hence they are not shown here but they are listed in the above book which runs almost to date and includes the Channel Islands and the Isle of Man – it starts at 1840 too!

THE ADHESIVE STAMPS ON POSTCARDS
1894–1939

It will be appreciated that only low denomination stamps were used on postcards therefore the normal stamp itself is almost valueless. However, there are many varieties in, the printing of the designs, the colours used, the perforations and watermarks, which are extremely valuable. A few of the highlights are listed here but those wishing to pursue the subject in greater depth MUST own or have access to, the necessary series of catalogues issued by Messrs. Stanley Gibbons Publications Ltd., 391, Strand, London WC2R 0LX.

1. *Stanley Gibbons Stamp Catalogue* Part 1 British Commonwealth 1980.

2. *The Great Britain Specialised Queen Victoria Catalogue* (5th edition October 1977).

3. *The Great Britain Edward VII to George VI ('Four Kings') Catalogue* (4th edition May 1978).

Postcard Postal Charges during the period (Inland)

1879 to June 1918 ½d.
June 1918 to June 1921 1d.
June 1921 to May 1922 1½d.
May 1922 to May 1940 1d.

Certain postcards treated as letters because of embellishments attracted the higher letter rate which was usually 50% higher but at times 100%. Postcards sent overseas were always 1d or more. These rates are the reasons for the low denomination stamps used.

Technical Terms

The only one to worry non-philatelists is 'perforation', but if you buy yourself a perforation gauge (I suggest one of the plastic transparent ones) you can ignore any technicalities and just use it (cost – a few pence to 50p or so depending upon quality). If a stamp is described as perf. 14 that means that on ALL four sides it will fit exactly on to your 14 gauge section. If it says 15 x 14 it means that the TOP and the BOTTOM perforations of the stamp will fit the 15 section on your gauge and the LEFT and RIGHT side perforations will fit the 14 section.

PERFORATION GAUGE

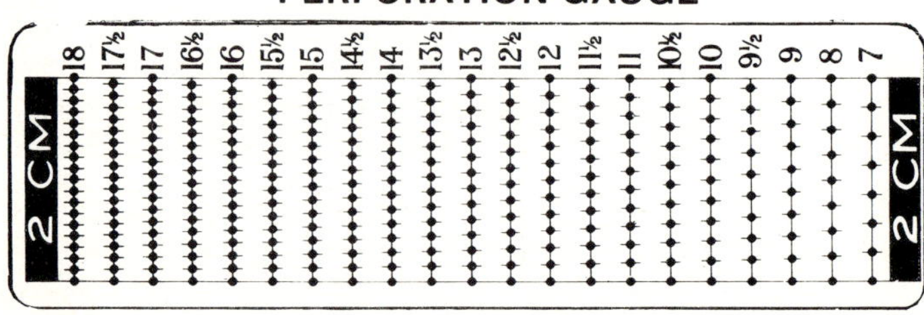

Watermarks and Markings made on the Back of Stamps

Although the books will show many stamps worth considerable sums if the watermark is found to be inverted etc. the only way to ascertain this is to 'sweat box' or wash the stamp off the postcard. This will almost certainly damage the postcard so that I do not envisage that many postcard collectors will go to the length of checking for watermarks and underprints (like Pear's Soap printed on the back, which, as an advertisement on Victorian ½d and 1d stamps is worth up to £300).
Colour, Perforation and Design variations can be detected without removal from the postcard hence the short list now shown.
Naturally all prices refer to used specimens but at times 'unused' stamps appear on postcards so that the necessary catalogues should be referred to for such stamps.
Most of the defects in the designs mentioned are illustrated in the catalogues quoted earlier. Remember that stamps can be hoarded and used many years later so watch for such late use (worth a premium).

ADHESIVE STAMPS

		Used Val.
Queen Victoria		
1d Lilac	(a) Design defect – 'broken frame' at bottom	£125
(16 dot)	(b) Design defect – right side of broken frame	£40
	(c) Bluish-lilac shade	£30
½d Vermillion	If issued without perforations (rare)	£100
½d Blue-green	If without perforations (rare)	£150

Note. The above stamps as normals catalogue at only 10p–12p which means that they are virtually unsellable.

King Edward VII		
½d Blue-green	Various split and broken frames	£1 to £5
½d Yellow-green	(a) Various split and broken frames	£1 to £10
	(b) With the printing at base of stamp showing partial or full doubling of design mint or unused	£1500
	used no data	?
	(c) With another stamp attached to it showing only a St. Andrew's Cross (used to fill up the spaces in booklets)	£90

½d Green On 3rd May 1911 Messrs. Harrisons took over the printing from Messrs. De La Rue using the same perf. 14. The printings were mainly blotchy and the date in the cancellation usually indicates the change of printers.

	Used Val.
(a) St. Andrew's Cross attached	£100
(b) Major Frame breaks and defects	£35
(c) A bright green, fine PRINTING OF June 1911	£100
(d) Deep bright green	£30
(e) Deep DULL yellow green (very blotchy)	£20

King Edward VII

½d Dull green (October 1911 - Harrison print) rarer perforation 15 x 14.

(a) Frame breaks	£50
(b) The normal stamp because of the 'mixed' 15 x 14	£6
(c) A deep dull green (very blotchy)	£35

1d 'Red' De La Rue up to May 1911 perf. 14

(a) Design defects (various)	£1 to £50
(b) The normal colour is scarlet so that a rose-carmine shade values at	£6

Harrison Perf. 14. dated from 3rd May 1911

(a) Frame breaks	£5
(b) Aniline rose	£65
(c) Aniline pink (there are other scarce shades).	£90

Harrison perf. 15 by 14 (instead of 14 by 14).

(a) Broken frame defects	£6
(b) Deep rose-red shade	£8
(c) Aniline pink (only 3 copies reported (Date around Dec. 1911) valued by Messrs. D.Forbes-Smith of Bristol in 1978 at over	£2,600

(This is S.G. No. 275 in the S.G. Commonwealth Catalogue but the 15 by 14 perf. instead of 14 all round is not listed as yet by S.G.)

George V 1911-1912

½d Green. Three Quarter Face

(a) Instead of usual 15 by 14 perf. - all round 14	£175
(b) BLUISH Green	£40
(c) No cross on crown	£10
(d) No cross on crown plus broken frame	£50

1d Red Three-Quarter Face with Lion Couchant beneath

(a) Perforation 14 all round (Mint £3,500) used - no data	?
(b) No cross on crown	£45
(c) Damaged crown and/or frame	£5 to £40
(d) Aniline Scarlet (June 1912 onwards)	£35

	Used Val.
George V 1912-22	
½d Green	
(full profile)	
(a) New Moon flaw	£85
(b) Deep Myrtle Green	£70
(c) Olive Green	£15
1d Red (no Lion)	
(a) Q for O in the one of 'one penny'	£60
(b) Shade of Pink	£40
(c) Deep Orange Vermillion (1918)	£40
1½d Brown	
(a) Brown	£70
(b) Pale Brown	£60
(c) The Pence Error (defective 'e' like an 'f')	£35 to £50
George V. 1924-26	
½d Green. Doubly printed	Mint £1250. Used?
1d Red Inverted Q for O in 'one'.	Mint £300. Used?
George V. Commemorative 1924-1935	
Wembley Exhibition	
1924 1d Scarlet	£9
1925 1d Scarlet	£15
'Tail' to N of Exhibition (1924 only)	£15
Postal Union Congress. 1929	
1½d Brown	
(a) Error 1829 for 1929	£40
(b) Q for O in union	£60
Edward VIII. 1936	
½d Green. Double Impression	£250

Note. Most of the varieties listed above if sent to a Philatelic Auction may be expected to realise, depending upon the quality of the stamp, from 25% to 75% of the figures indicated as the *popularity* of the 'variety' *at the moment* is the true test of value.

OVERSEAS STAMPS

Colonial and Foreign Stamps on postcards, including postmarks

This is a vast subject. Loose stamps, i.e. stamps off postcard (or envelope) can be priced by the many catalogues on the market especially those from Messrs Stanley Gibbons Ltd, but postcards from abroad bearing 'foreign' stamps are a problem. Most of the stamps are of low denomination being regular issues usually of no real commercial value but some of the pictorial stamps may, here and there, have value.

However, such is the popularity of postal history today that the 20th century used postcard is now much sought after. Pricing becomes a problem. If the value of the picture side exceeds that of the postmark and/or stamp value, now to be indicated, then that aspect should naturally take price precedence (you do not add the different values together, you must settle for the value of the picture or the address side).

We are dealing with stamps mainly from around 1900 to 1939 and naturally the older the stamps the more likely they are to be of value – that is a generalistation and this section can only generalise for a vast field.

COLONIAL PRICING

Dominions etc

Australia, Canada, New Zealand, South Africa and India, have large populations so that most cards are very common, i.e. the *stamps* thereon, so rarely more than 15p to 25p (The picture side is usually worth more).

Small Colonies

Solely because of the small populations, philatelists pay quite well for the smaller Crown Colonies, especially the islands, when bearing the stamps of such territories. It is hard to generalise but the commoner and larger of these, and those better known, and those nearer to Britain, like Malta, and Gibraltar value at £1 to £2.

The more distant colonies like the West Indies, St. Helena and Seychelles price from £2 to £5 and the Falkland Islands rise to £10 or more. The Pacific Islands value up well too (£2 to £5).

OVERSEAS STAMPS

Foreign Countries

Europe

France, Germany, Italy, Belgium, Holland, Switzerland, Spain, Portugal, are countries with large populations and therefore the stamps are common. The picture side is almost always likely to exceed the value of the stamps thereon.

The smaller States of Europe like Iceland, Greece, the Baltic States, Andorra, are worth a premium, say 50p, and here and there up to £2.

The Russian postcards with Czarist or Soviet stamps thereon seem very popular, fetching now from £1 to £2, and even more from remote towns (if you can read the Russian!). The Irish Free State, using G.B. stamps overprinted, are very popular, £1 to £2, even though they are of low denomination.

Africa

European colonies, French, Portuguese, Spanish, Belgian - some demand - £1 to £2.

Liberia, Ethiopia, very popular, up to £5. North African States, including Egypt, less popular £1.

Asia

India, China, Japan, no premium, too common. The smaller states, expecially around the Persian Gulf fare better, 50p to £2.

Palestine, Thailand, Dutch East Indies are better, upwards of £5. Hejaz, if you ever see one, £10.

America

The U.S.A. and Latin America. Either the populations are too large or the countries unpopular, philatically speaking. Rarely any premium. However, some of the smaller Latin American states command a small 50p to £1 premium, like Haiti, Cuba, Ecuador, Costa Rica. Hawaii and Puerto Rico are worthy of a £1 to £2 premium.

British Post Office - Constantinople - Price £5.

OVERSEAS POSTAL MARKINGS

We have, so far, been considering *only* the adhesive stamp applied to the post-card. When we come to cancellations and other postal markings there is a different story to tell. Rarer postmarks such as those connected with Transport i.e. Paquebot or Rail can fetch substantial figures often up to £25 in our period. Most markings can be equated with those for Britain, namely common slogans are not in much demand but Travelling Post Offices, although common, are collected and fetch premiums of £2 or so, especially the German ones.

Japanese cards with 'unreadable' cachets (usually circular in shape) fetch £2 premiums or more. On the other hand, German colonial stamps used in China, Africa or the Pacific always command premiums of up to £5 or more, just for the normal cancellation.

It is a vast subject, too vast for a catalogue of this nature but this section should alert you to the potential value of Overseas cards and if you want to sell them to best advantage put them into a Philatelic Auction in small batches and you will be agreeably surprised (and that goes for the foreign and colonial stamped cards, too, but not so much likelihood of a windfall there). A few examples are illustrated in this catalogue with prices.

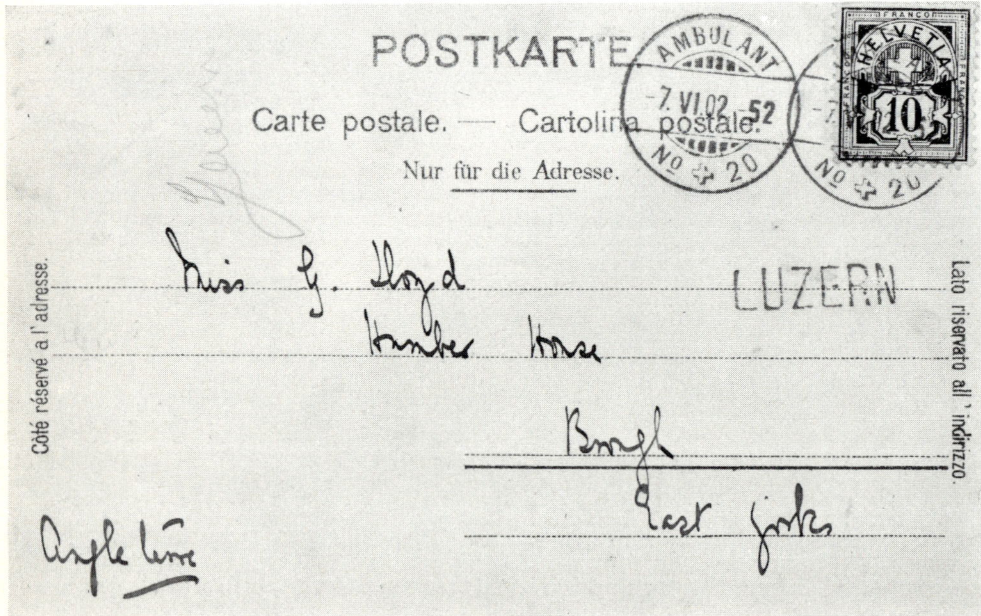

Postcard Clubs

American Postcard Club Federation (40 societies approx.)
Director Box 27 Somerdale, New Jersey 08083 U.S.A.

Avon Postcard Club. (Countrywide membership accepted)
Marion Freeman, 24 Cherry Orchard, Pershore, Worcs.

Bedfordshire Postcard Club
Warden Hill, Community Centre behind Warden Tavern Public House, Luton, Beds.

Bradford & District Postcard Society.
A. E. Wood, 26 Front View, Shelf, Halifax.

Cambridge Univ. Deltiologists.
Mr. M. Ellison, Clare College, Cambridge, U.K.

Great Britain, Postcard Club of
Mrs. D. Brennan, 34 Harper House, St. James's Crescent,
London SW9 7DW

Herts. Postcard Club.
Neil Jenkins, 113 Bramble Rd., Hatfield, Herts.

Huddersfield & District Postcard Society.
Mr. G. Wolstenholme, 13 Westroyd Park, Mirfield, West Yorks.

Irish Picture Postcard Society
Cathair Books, T. D. Rose, Secretary. South Ding St., Dublin 2.

Leeds Postcard Club.
Mrs. A. Whitelock, 9 Brentwood Grove, Leeds, Yorks. LS12 2DB

Lincoln Collectors Club.
T. G. Collier, 2 Wickenby Close, North Hykeham, Lincoln.

London Postcard Club.
Joyce Cohen, 58 Sandringham Rd., London NW11.

Maidstone Postcard Club.
Mrs. I. Hales, 40 Hildenborough Crescent, Maidstone.

Mercia Postcard Club.
Maurice L. Palmer, 5 Saxon Rise, Earls Barton, Northants. NN6 0NY.

Newcastle-upon-Tyne Postcard Club.
Mrs. M. Osbourne, 26 Balmoral Terrace, South Gosforth,
Newcastle-upon-Tyne NE3 1YH.

Norfolk Postcard Club.
Mr. P.J.Standley, 63 Folly Rd., Wymondham, Norfolk.

North of England Postcard Club.
F.A.Fletcher, 35 St. Georges Terrace, East Bolden, Tyne & Wear.

Rushden, Northants.
Mr. B.Church, 2 Meadow Drive, Higham Ferrers NN9 8EZ
or Mr. E.Fowell, 101 Spencer Rd., Rushden, Northants.

Somerset.
Mr. D.Burgess, 55 Waterloo Rd., Wellington, Somerset.

Suffolk Postcard Club.
Mrs. Peggy Southgate, 8 The Green, Mistley, Manningtree, Essex.

Sussex Postcard Club.
Dave Bull, 12 The Broadway, Lancing.

Tees Valley Collectors Club.
A.J.Lambert, 15 Glenfield Road, Darlington, Co. Durham.

Warrington & District Postcard Club.
Mrs. J.Fisher, 63 Slater Street, Latchford, Warrington, Cheshire.

NOTICE TO SOCIETY SECRETARIES

If Secretaries will write to us with details of new societies and changes of personnel and/or addresses we will publish them in the next edition.

Cachet - Defeat of Russia by Japan - Price £15.

SOME MAGAZINES FOR THE PICTORIAL POSTCARD COLLECTOR

CLASSIC ERA

Refer to the *Catalogue of the Philatelic Library of The Earl of Crawford, K.T.* by E.D. Bacon 1911 (London–Philatelic Literature Society). It lists to 1908 almost all known philatelic periodicals, many of which contained considerable postcard reference or were *wholly devoted* to postcards. I quote:-

(a) *The Collectors' News* (or I.P.R. & Collectors News) 1902–3
(b) *Postal Cards & Covers,* Leeds (1900–01) (E.D. Wilson)
(c) *The Picture Postcard,* London (E.D. Richardson) 1900–1903
(d) *The Collectors' Advertiser* (later *Magazine* later *Journal*) 1901–1907. Published in Rotherham called initially *Universal Advertiser*

MODERN POSTCARD MAGAZINES

1. *Postcard World* (Organ of the Postcard World Club, a British National Society) Published by Mrs. D. Brennan, 34, Harper House, St James Crescent, Brixton, London SW9 7LW.
2. *Deltiology* (Published by James L.Lowe, U.S.A.)
3. *Collectors Market* (Published J.H.D.Smith, Kingscote Station, East Grinstead, Sussex.
4. *Postcard Collectors Gazette* (Published by Postcard Collectors Gazette Ltd., 36 Asmuns Hill, London NW11 6ET)
5. *Transy News* (Published by H. Richardson, 27B, Marchmont Rd., Edingburgh EH9 1HY).
6. *The Postcard Collectors Guide* (Published by A. J. Butland, 32 Merton Avenue, Upper Stratton, Swindon, Wiltshire SN2 6PY).
7. *The Postcard Mail* (Published by Bray-Rhodes Doughty, P.O. Box 39, Loughborough, Leics.
8. Reflections of a Bygone Age (Published at 27 Walton Drive, Keyworth, Notts).
9. *The Exchange and Mart*, Link House, Dingwall Avenue, Croydon CR9 2TA. It contains only advertisements but carries more for postcards than most other productions.
10. *La Cartophile*, organ of the Cercles Francais des Collectioneurs de Carte Postals, 117 Bd. Saint Germain, Paris 6, France. (Open to membership application).
11. *Hertfordshire Postcard Magazine*, Ron Griffiths, 47 Long Arrotts, Hemel Hempstead MP1 3EX.

SOME MAGAZINES FOR THE PHILATELIST AND WITH MUCH TO INTEREST THE POSTCARD COLLECTOR

1. *Philatelic Magazine* (Published every 15th of the month) address as for Stamp Collecting Weekly - see below.
2. *Stamp Collecting Weekly,* 42 Maiden Lane, London WC2E 7LL (Published weekly on Thursdays).
3. *Stamp Magazine* (Published monthly last day of each month) Link House, Dingwall Avenue, Croydon CR9 2TA.
4. *Stamp Monthly* (A Stanley Gibbons Magazine) (Published monthly Drury House, Russell Street, London WC2B 5HD)
5. *Stamp Lover* (A quarterly from the National Philatelic Society, 1, Whitehall Place, London SW1A 2HE).
6. *The Philatelic Intelligencer*, 187 Lichfield Road, Stone, Staffs ST15 8QB.
7. *Philately*, B.P.E., 1 Whitehall Place, London SW1A 2HE.

SOME HANDBOOKS TO HELP THE PHILATELIST AND THE COLLECTOR OF GOVERNMENT PRODUCED POSTCARDS

See under the appropriate 'Postmark' sections for the handbook(s) your compiler considers the most useful in each case. There are many other books that could be mentioned which space does not allow but the following just must be quoted:-

1. Robson Lowe Ltd. Encyclopedia Vols I–V.
2. Higgins & Gage. *Priced Catalogue of Postal Stationery of the World* (G.B. Section (1967) is Part 7) - Pasadena, California, U.S.A.
3. Huggins, A.K. *British Postal Stationery* (1970) Published by the Great Britain Philatelic Society.

BIBLIOGRAPHY

SOME MAINLY MODERN HANDBOOKS TO HELP THE POSTCARD COLLECTOR

Alderson, F. - *The Comic Postcard in English Life* 1970

Andrews, B. - *A Directory of Postcards, Artists, Publishers and Trademarks.* An American production covering the World 1975.

Bernard, I. and W. - *Picture Postcard Catalogue - Germany 1870–1945*-Priced (In English, French & German) (current).

Bernard, I and W. *Special Picture Postcard Catalogue - National Socialism 1933–45* Priced. (In English, French & German) 1976.

Bowers, F. & Jaeger, K. *Greetings from Bath* Kingsmead Press, Bath 1977

Buday, George, A.R.E - *The Story of the Christmas Card* (1951) Odhams Press Ltd. London.

Burdick, J.R. - *The American Card Catalogue* (The Standard Guide to all Collected cards and their values 1967). Every type of card **except** postcards i.e. includes passing references to postcards only, strong on Trade Cards - The American scene.

Burdick J.R. - *Pioneer Postcards* (the story of mailing cards to 1898) with an illustrated check list of publishers and titles. Whole World (reprinted recently). Originally printed 1956.

Burdick J.R. - *A Directory of the 'Detroits'* in the collection of,

Butland, A.J. and Westwood, E.A. - *Picture Postcards and All about Them* Printed Rutherdale Stationery Co. Ltd. Teddington, Middlesex. (Includes the first G.B. Priced Catalogue of Pictorial Postcards of modern time c. 1960)

Byatt, A. - *Picture Postcards and their Publishers*, 1978.

Bystander, The. *Bairnsfather* (192?)

Calder-Marshal, A. - *The Art of Donald McGill* Selected and Appraised by, 1966.

Campbell, G. and Schoeller, A. *Catalogue des Cartes Postales (1889)* in French.

Carline, Richard - *Pictures in the Post* (1959) Gordon Frazer Ltd. Bedford. (Revd. Ed. 1971). (Contains a fine bibliography at the commencement of the book).

Carver, Sally S. *Tuck* (American Postcard guide to 'Tuck' Cards, Massachusetts 1976)

Duval, W. & Monahan, Valerie. *Collecting Postcards in colour.* (Blandford Press Dorset 1978)

Fildier, Argus - *Cartes Postales Anciennes de Collection* (annually). Fine French Catalogue - Priced. French Scene.

Filnkobl, H. *100 Jähre Postkarte* (1973)

Fletcher, F.A. and Brooks, A.D. - *British Exhibitions and Their Postcards. Part 1 1900-1914*

Frech, H. - Private Postcard Catalogue (in German). Priced - Special Events c. 1975.

Freeman, L. Dr. *Wish you were here* Century House, New York 14891 (1976)

Fronval, F. - *Catalogue Imagerie Bon Marche* deals with all the Trade Cards of the House of "Bon Marche", in Paris. (no date). (no valuations).

Fumagalli, Luigi - *Catalogo Internazionale delle Cromo-Litografie Liebig* (Fada). Third Edition with supplements 1957. Fully Priced, deals with all the Liebig Trade Cards.

Guyonnet, George - *La Carte Postale Illustree. Son Histoire, Sa Valeur Documentaire.* Edited by the Chambre Syndicale Francaise de la Carte Postale Illustree, c. 1946. The French scene.

Hammond, P. - *French Undressing* - 1976

Hill, C. W. - *Discovering Picture Postcards* (1970) Shire Publications (Tring).

Holt, Valmi and Toni *Picture Postcards of the Golden Age, Collectors Guide* 1971. Fine Production (splendid research) (being reprinted now)

Holt, Valmi and Toni *Till the Boys come Home: The Picture Postcards of the First World War* published by Macdonald & Jane's - 1977

Janssens, L *Catalogue des Chromos Liebig (1933)*

Kaduck, J.M. - *Mail Memories (Pictorial Guide to Postcard Collecting)* with prices. Highly illustrated. American scene. 1971.

Lawrence, P.N. *Picture Postcard 1870-1920* A Brochure relating to the Travelling Exhibition arranged by the Circulation Dept. of the Victoria and Albert Museum of Postcards contributed to the Exhibition by the Author, Mr. P.N. Lawrence.

Lawrence, P.N. *The Social Significance of the Picture Postcard* (1975)

Lauterbach & Jokovsky - *A Picture Postcard Album*, published by Thomas & Hudson (1961).

Lewis, John - *Printed Ephemera 1969.* English and American printing through the ages. Unpriced.

Lowe, J.L. - *Lincoln Postcard Catalogue, 1967.* All the cards associated with President Lincoln. Priced.

Lowe, J.L. - *A Bibliography of Postcard Literature 1969.*

Lowe, J.L. & Papell, B. *Detroit Publishing Company Collectors' Guide* (1975)

Lowe, J.L. - *Standard Postcard Catalogue* Better Postcard Collectors' Club, Gradyville, P.A., U.S.A. (First Edition 1968)

Mackay, James A. - *Scottish Postmarks* (1978) 11, Newhall Terrace, Dumfries.

Miller, D and G. *Picture Postcards in the United States 1893-1918* (Clarkson N. Potter. New York (1976)

Neudin, J. - *Cartes Postales de Collection.* A fine annual Catalogue (in French). Priced. French scene

Norgaard, Eirk. *With Love* Published by MacGibbon & Nee London 1969

O'Reilly, Patrick - *Centenaire de la Carte Postale (1871-1970).* 1970

Ouellete, W. - *Fantasy Postcards* (1975).

Radley, C. - *History of Silk Postcards* (1975) (First listing of embroidered cards as well as woven - scarcity graded too).

Radley, C. - *Collecting Silk Postcards* (1976)

Radley, C. - *The Embroidered Silk Postcard* (1977)

Radley, C. - *The Woven Silk Postcard* (1978)

Scott, W.J. - *All about Postcards 1903.* A fine *contemporary* handbook in the hey day of the *Edwardian* postcard craze.

Scherer, R.W. *Bamforth Checklist* Parts (1) 1973 and (2) 1973

Smith, J. (I.P.M.) - *A Priced Catalogue of Picture Postcards.* A fine catalogue by an eminent British Dealer. An 'Annual' production.

Sprake, A.M.A. and Darby, M. - *Stevengraphs* (1968). Printed by Fletcher & Son Ltd., Norwich and the priced guide of 1971.

Staff, Frank - *The Picture Postcard and its Origins* (1966), Lutterworth Press. (A most erudite production). Highly recommended and also for the philatelically inclined.

Staff, Frank - *The Valentine and its Origins* (1969).
Welsh, Roger, L. *Tall-Tale Postcards.* A.S. Barnes & Co. New Jersey, 08512 (1976).
Wolstenholme, George - *ABC of Postcard Collecting* (1973)
Wolstenholme, George. *Peeps into the Postcard Past* (1974)

N.B. Most of the *Catalogues* listed above are repeated at intervals (not always annually) so check for the latest date when buying.
AUTHORS, EDITORS or ANYONE please advise us of any titles we have omitted, for inclusion, if space allows, in future editions.

Publisher's Note
Some words of foreign origin throughout this catalogue have been Anglicised, deliberately, by omitting accents and similar marks.

Persia (Iran) - Price £3.

SOURCES OF SUPPLY

1. The advertisers in this Catalogue (many with retail shops or stalls working to regular opening hours).
2. The Auctions (both Postal and Public) listed in this Catalogue.
3. Many of the advertisers to be found in the modern magazines shown under "Magazines" in this Catalogue.
4. The *Lists* issued by Retailers shown in this Catalogue under "Auctions and Lists".
5. Apply for membership of a Postcard Club listed in this Catalogue and/or the Local Stamp Society listed in The B.P.A. Philatelic Societies Directory from the British Philatelic Federation Ltd., 1, Whitehall Place, London SW1 2HE. (revised annually).
(You will always find many postcard enthusiasts in stamp clubs to-day as the hobbies are now very complementary).
6. **Retail Shops.** There are very few devoted *solely* to selling postcards but of these many will be found listed in this Catalogue. Any dealer who would like to be listed in future Catalogues is invited to send us details of the shop address with days and hours of business but in the meantime we are not listing specific shops because hours of opening are usually so indefinite (because of early closing and the fact that shops are closed whilst the firm takes part in 'Fairs' and not forgetting change of address, emigration, holidays and just 'closing down'). However for the intrepid we suggest you get a copy of the directory quoted at the end of this section which lists most of the stamp dealers/shops in the World. In any area if you visit its local stamp shops no doubt some cards will be available there and the proprietors will be able also to provide the address of other postcard dealers in the area. In the absence of data from this source try the antique shops till one of them puts you on to the person who 'does' cards in a big way in the area.
7. Finally watch the local and specialist media for details of Fairs in your area (Stamp, Book, Coin, etc. - there are usually postcards too).

International Stamp Dealers' Directory
Published by Harris Publications 42 Maiden Lane, Strand, London WC2.
(This lists nearly 1,000 stamp dealers in the British Isles and 1,000's more throughout the World).

A LIST OF SPECIALIST POSTCARD DEALERS AND ALSO PHILATELIC AUCTIONEERS AND/OR LIST ISSUERS, WHOSE CATALOGUES AND/OR LISTS CONTAIN MANY OR A FEW POSTCARD LOTS

Note. Please read all the advertisements first as their inserters are positively in business and have paid to put details in this Catalogue but some may not be repeated here so read ALL the adverts to ensure you miss no one and if you do business with any of these firms you might mention you found the name and address in this catalogue. A few foreign addresses are included.

We cannot be sure whether some names listed have shops or not, nor, if they do, we do not know their opening hours. When in doubt telephone or write them before calling and to avoid entering incorrect information we have used (   ) as below.

Abbreviations Used
(A) means Auction (Postal or Public)
(F) Fair or Market
(L) means List
(PCL) means mainly Postcard List
(PCA) means mainly Postcard Auction
(S) means Shop (or regular Stall in a 'regular Centre')
(   ) means Dealer but method of trading not known to compiler.

IMPORTANT
If any person or company trades in postcards from a shop or market or has a postal business and issues lists and/or is open to the public, *regularly*, we shall be happy to list, free, such addresses if space allows, in future issues of this edition or in future annual editions. Please notify us.

Any errors of commission or omission, will be rectified in future if readers will kingly advise the Publishers.

Alcock, R. C., Ltd. 11, Regent Street, Cheltenham, Glos. GL50 1HJ (L)

Alexander Galleries, 81, Station Parade, Harrogate HG1 1S (S) (PCL)

'Alucards', 42 Sinclair Drive, Glasgow G42 9QE
Tel. 041-649 0115 (PCL)

Ark Stamps, 18, Hockley, Nottingham NG1 1FP (L)

Armada, (B. G. Skinner) 15, Surrey Street,
Brighton BN1 3PA (A) (PCA) (S)

Barefoot, J., Ltd., 85, Saltergate, Chesterfield S40 1JS (L)

Barnes, T.G., Duncan Chambers, 9 Duncan St., Leeds 1. (A)

Bath Collectors Centre, (B.Swallow)
Gt. Western Antique Centre, Bath (S)

Bath Stamp & Coin Shop, 12, Pulteney Bridge, Bath (S)

Beckenham Stamp Centre, 1 Station Approach, West Wickham,
Kent. (A) (S)

Bendon, James P.O. Box 673, London SW13 0EJ (Philatelic) (L)

Bennett, C "Giffords", Ursula Avenue, Selsey, Sussex (L)

Bennett, Messrs., 7, Franklin Close,
Worcester WR2 4DX (A) (L) (PCL) (PCA)

Birmingham Stamp Co.
104 Sherbourne Avenue, Bucks Hill, Nuneaton, Warwicks. CV10 9JL (A)

Boite Postale, (La) Case Postale 29, CH-1008, Prilly, Switzerland (A)

Bolton Stamp Auctions, Bradford Buildings, 27 Mawdsley St., Bolton (A)

Bournemouth Stamp Auctions, 39 Poole Hill, Bournemouth BH2 5PX (A)

Bridger & Kay, 86, Strand, London WC2 (A)

Brittania Stamp Bureau, 21, Broomhill Rd., Tiverton, Devon EX16 5AR (L)

Byatt, A, 28 St. Peter's Rd., Malvern, Worcs (PCL)

Cambridgeshire Philatelic Auctions, The, 5 Market St. Ely, Cambs. (A)

Capital Philatelic Auctions, P.O. Box 18, Middlesex TW11 9JY (A)

Carey, Aubrey, Spire Stamps, 144 Chester St., Chesterfield, Derbyshire ( )

Carson, W., 42 Park Circus, Ayr KA7 2DL (A)

Cavendish Philatelic Auctions,
Progressive Buildings, Sitwell St., Derby. (A) (S)

Centurion Stamp Company
20 Wellowgate, Grimsby, S. Humberside (PCL) (S)
Chamberlain, Desmond P.O. Box 725, London SW15 3R (PCL)

City of London Philatelic Auctions Ltd., 170, Bishopsgate,
London EC2 (A)

Classic Philatelic Auctions, 28, Lower Street, Chagford, Devon (A)

Collectors Mail Auctions, (PTY) Ltd.,
P.O. Box 20, Bergvliet, Cape, South Africa. (A)

Cornish Stamp Company, 1 Dobbin Lane, Trevone, Cornwall (A)

Crest Collectors Centre, Mid-Kent Shopping Centre,
Allington, Maidstone (closed Wed. afternoons) (S)

Dacorum Stamp Auctions, 49 High Acres, Abbots Langley, Herts. (A)

Dauwalder, P.S. & A. 53, Fisherton Street, Salisbury, Wilts. (L) (S)

Davis, Stuart,
1, Hibernia Mansions, Victoria Quadrant,
Weston-super-Mare BS23 2QB (PCL)

Davis, Trevor P.O. Box 727, London SW20 0RP (L)

Desiderata Postfach 5362 D78 Friedburg BRD (West Germany) ( )

Doig, Kerr 58, Hopetoun Street, Bathgate, Scotland (A)

Dorchester Stamp Shop (K. S. Summers),
5, Tudor Arcade, South Street, Dorchester, Dorset DT1 1BN (S)

East Anglian Stamp Auctions, P.O. Box 15, Colchester,
Essex CO3 2BR (A)

East of England Philatelic Auctions, 53/65, Ledbury St.,
Peterboro' (A)

Edinburgh Stamp Shop, 145, Buccleugh St., Edinburgh EH8 9NE (A) (S)

Elm Hill Stamp Auctions, 27, Elm Hill, Norwich, Norfolk (A)

Felpham Stamp Auctions, 94 Felpham Road, Felpham,
Bognor Regis, West Sussex. (A)

F.P. Auctions, 'Keren', St. Aubyns Gardens, Orpington, Kent. (A)

Field, David, Ltd., 42 Berkeley St., Mayfair, London W1X 5FP (S) (L)

Field, Francis J., Ltd.,
Richmond Road, Sutton Coldfield, W. Midlands B73 6BJ (L)

Fisher, 63 Slater Street, Latchford, Warrington, Chesire WA4 1DN ( )

Forbes-Smith, D., 12 Christmas Steps, Bristol BS1 5BS (Philatelic) (L)

Foster, G. (Mrs) 14 Shortley Road, Coventry, Warwicks CV3 4AE (PCL)

Franks, J.A.L., 180, Fleet Street, London EC4 (S)

Franks, 22 Bond Street, Brighton (S)

Franks, Laurie, Ltd., Christchurch 1, New Zealand, (Private Bag) (A)

Globe International, 1 Crosby St., Carlisle, Cumbria (S) (A)

Graham, Conrad, 23 Rotherwick Road, London NW11 7DG Literature (A)

Green, D.L. Sticklands Farm, East Morden, Wareham,
Dorset DH20 7DL (L)

Griffiths, Ron., 47, Long Arrotts, Hemel Hempstead, Herts HP1 3EX (PCL)

Grosvenor, R, 18 New Rd., Abbey Wood, London, SE2 ( )

H.J.M.R., P.O. Box 610308, North Miami, Florida-33161, U.S.A.(A) Literature

Harmer, H.R., Ltd., 41 New Bond Street, London W1A 4EH. (A)

Harris Publications Ltd., 42 Maiden Lane, Strand,
London WC (S) Literature

Hayes, Harry, 48, Trafalgar Street, Healey, Batley,
Yorks. WF17 7HA (A) Literature

Hislop, R. M., Ltd., 7 High Street, Linlithgow, West Lothian (A)

Hopkins Auctions, The Square, Porth, Mid-Glamorgan CF39 9SU (A)

Hunt, D & F.,
White Lodge Woodlands Close, Gerrards Cross,
Bucks. SL9 8DQ (Philatelic)(L)

Hutchinson, J., 17A North Parade, Bradford 1, Yorkshire (PCL)

Hyde, Rikki, 10, Lower Ashley Road, Bristol 2 (A) (S) (PCA)

I.B.B. Auctioneers 55/57 Albert Street, Rugby CV21 2SG. (A)

I.P.M. Ltd. (J.D.Smith),, Kingscote Station,
East Grinstead, Sussex (L)

International Stamp Auctions (Myers Stamps),
4 York Place, Leeds LS1 2DR (A)

Jackson, Alex, 81 Station Parade, Harrogate, North Yorks. HG1 1ST ( )

Jeremy's, 98 Cowley Road, Oxford. Tel. 41011 ( )

Jones, G. Peter, 16 Winterton Way, Shoreham-by-Sea,
Sussex BN4 5RE (L)

Kirkland, B., 6 Todwell Lane, Little Horton, Bradford ( )

Kretschmer, 19 The Crossways, Wembley, Middlesex HA9 9NG ( )

Lancastrian Philatelic Auctions,
41 Severn Drive, Walton-le-Dale, Preston PR5 4TD (A)

Langton, Garnet, Burlington Arcade, Bournemouth (S)

Lawson, K. Middlesex Collectors Centre,
24 Watford Road, Sudbury, Wembley, Middlesex (S) (PCA)

Leeds Card Centre, 41/43 Bregate, Leeds LS1 6NO
(Open Mon, Tues, Thurs, Fri) (S)

Legg, Faith (Miss) Hill House, Victoria Hill, Eye, Suffolk (S)

Leicester Philatelic Auctions Ltd., Northampton Sq., Leicester (A)

London Postcard Centre, 21, Kensington Park Rd., London W.11. (Stalls)

London Stamp Exchange Ltd., 5, Buckingham St., Strand WC2N 6BS (A)

Loth, Gunter, Neubrunnenstr-12-6500, Mainz, West Germany (A)

Lund, B., 27, Walton Drive, Keyworth, Notts. (PCL)

Magpies, Great Withey Bush, Knowle Lane, Cranleigh, Surrey (PCL)

McCreedy, 6 Castle Drive, Richill, Armagh (PCL)

Meads Antiques, 9, Meads Street, Eastbourne ( )

Mercia International Auctions Ltd., 22 Regent Place, Rugby, Warwicks (A)

Michaels, 10a, St. Stephens Lane, Ipswich, Suffolk ( )

Midland Stamp Company, P.O. Box 22308 Memphis,
Tennessee 38122, U.S.A. (A)

Mundel, G., Shop 8, Malthouse Antique Market, Hythe, Kent (S)

Murchie, Duncan, Blue Horizons, Strete, Dartmouth, Devon TQ6 0RH (A)

Murray, 76, Barnet Way, Mill Hill, London NW7 3AN ( )

Neales of Nottingham, 192 Mansfield Road,
Nottingham NG1 3HX (PCA)

Norfolk Stamp Co., 33 Timberhill Common, Norwich NR1 3LO ( )

N.W.P. (North Western Philatelic Auctions Ltd.)
West Kirby, Wirral, Merseyside (A)

Past Delights, 1 Chapel Street, Guildford, Surrey GU1 3UH (S)

Pecourt, Edouard, 58, rue du Louvre, 75002, Paris ( )

Philhatelist, 141 Meersbrook Park Road, Sheffield S8 9FP ( )

Phillips, Messrs. Blenstock House,
7 Blenheim Street, New Bond Street, London W1Y 0AS (A)

Plumridge & Co., 6, Adam Street, Strand, London WC2N 6AA (A)

Portsmouth Stamp Shop, 184 Chichester Road, North End,
Portsmouth, Hants. (S)

Postal History International,
25 Meeting House Lane, Brighton BN1 1JS (S) (A)

Premier Stamp Auctions (T. N. Eley),
29, Howard Ave., Bedford MK40 4EE (A)

Presland Postcards, P.O. Box 38, Basingstoke, Hants. ( )

Provincial Philatelic Auctions, D. F. Holloway, Pinecroft,
Langley Hill, Calcot, Reading, Berks. RG3 5QU (A)

Radley, C., 20 Coombes Road, Dagenham, Essex RM9 6UL (L)

R. F. Postcards, 17, Hilary Crescent, Rayleigh, Essex (L) (PCL)

Rhodes-Doughty Postcards,
The Bays, Swing Bridge Road, Loughborough, Leics. (PCL)

Richardson, H., Transy News, 27B Marchmont Rd.,
Edinburgh EH9 1HY. (S) (L)

Roberts, G., 41, Glengall Road, Bexleyheath, Kent ( )

Robson Lowe Ltd., 50, Pall Mall, London SW1Y 5JZ (A)

Saddington, R. E., 156 Tuckton Rd., Tuckton,
Bournemouth BH6 3JX (A) (S)

Scene Before, (E.McKercher) P.O. Box 23
Bedford MK41 8BR (L)

Select Stamps, P.O. Box 20, Northampton (A)

Shapland, R. & C., The Stamp Shop, 13 Cross Street, Barnstaple,
North Devon (S)

Shelron Postcards, 18 New Road, Abbey Wood, London SE2. (F)

Shelron Auctions, 6 Beechill Road, Eltham SE9 1HH (A)

Simioni, Jean-Georges,
29, Rue du General, Kessayre, 47000 Agen, France (PCL)

Smith, R., 82, Stoneyfields Lane, Edgware, Middlesex HA8 9SR (PCL)

Solent Enterprises, Fourways, Church Hill, West End, Southampton. ( )

Southampton Philatelic Auctions,
27 Portsmouth Road, Woolston (A)

South Eastern Philatelic Auctions, P.O. Box 1, Cranbrook, Kent (A)

Stanley Gibbons, Drury House, Russel St., London WC2B 5H (A) (S)

Steyn, A. (Recollections), 5 Ludlow Way, London N.2. (PCL)

Swindon & Kennet Stamp Company,
78 Commercial Rd., Swindon, Wilts. SN1 5PD (S)

Taviner's Auction Rooms, Prewett St., Redcliffe, Bristol BS1 6PB. (A)

Tonge, Alan, 70, Birch Rd., Rixton, Warrington W13 6JS. ( )

Topical Stamps, 72 Moss Lane, Alderley Edge, Cheshire SK9 7HN. (L)

Townsend, M., 8 Netley Dell, Letchworth, Herts SG6 2TF (Phil. L)

Trevarn Railway Postal Auctions,
T.J.Cook, 42 Forest Way, Highcliffe, Christchurch, Dorset, BH23 4PZ (A)

Vale, 21, Tranquil Vale, Blackheath SE3 0BU. (S)

Vera Trinder Ltd., 38 Bedford St., Strand, London W.C. (S) Literature

Vessey Auctions, Bank House, High Street, Whitstable, Kent (A)

Vessoul Philatelie, 7, Rue de Breuil, 70000 Vesoul, France (S) (L)

Walter, Stephen, 109, Kingsley Rd., Hounslow, Middlesex TW3 4AL (A)

Warr, Tony, 136 Whitehorns Way, Drayton, Abingdon, Oxon
OX14 4LH (PCL)

Webb, Gordon & Honor,
53 Twinbrook Park, Swanpool, Falmouth, Cornwall. (Tel. 311978) (PCL)

Welton, Charles H.,
9 Mill Beck Lane, Cottingham, N. Humberside HU16 4ET (A)

Western Auctions Ltd.,
P.A. Wilde, Bank House, 225 City Road, Cardiff, Wales (A)

Westgate Philatelic Auctions,
13 Cross Street, Barnstaple, North Devon EX31 1BD (A)

West London Auctions, 295 High Street, Hounslow, Middlesex (PCA)

Whyte, Ian, 3 Fitzwilliam Place, Dublin 2, Ireland (L)

Williams, John, 30 Parksway, Woolston, Warrington ( )

Winchester Stamp Centre, 6b Parchment Street, Winchester, Hants (S)

Wolstenholme, G.
Villa Rose, 13, Westroyd Park, Mirfield, Yorks. WF14 9NA (PCL)

Woodall, F.G., Forest Cottage, Holtwood, Wimbourne,
Dorset BH21 7DT (callers Tel. Witchampton 203 *first*) (PCL)

Worth, Kiki, 15 Corinne Road, London N19. (PCL)

Worthing Stamp Auctions, 25 West Buildings, Worthing (A)

York Stamp Exchange, 63 Micklegate, York (S)

Foreign Sources. There are so many dealers in every country nowadays that it is not possible to list them ALL here. If you wish to deal with a particular country I suggest you buy the Postcard Catalogues listed in this catalogue for the U.S.A., Germany and France or get a copy of the International Stamp Dealers' Directory – these days nearly all stamp dealers dabble in postcards and can put you on to other sources in their country if you go visiting there. The U.S.A. market is now enormously developed (they have 5 times our population) with many postcard auctions, magazines, fairs, exhibitions and dealers far in excess of even our own highly active market.

Danzig – Price £2.

APPENDIX 1
The Evolution of the Postcard (1869–1918)

1st Oct. 1869	First postcard issued (World's first)
1st Oct. 1870	G.B. issued her first postcard.
1st April 1872	G.B. privately printed postcards allowed.
9th Oct. 1874	First meeting of the Universal Postal Union.
1st July 1875	G.B. issued her first 1¼d postcard for foreign use.
1st April 1879	G.B. issued two new foreign postcards.
1st May 1882	First exhibition postcard issued (Nuremberg)
1st Oct. 1882	G.B. first reply postcard issued.
1st Sept. 1894	Privately printed postcards for use with adhesive stamps allowed in G.B.
1894	First British picture postcard issued by Messrs. Geo. Stewart.
21st Jan. 1895	First official court size card issued in G.B.
16th June 1897	Writing on address side of a postcard no longer forbidden by the G.P.O.
1st Nov. 1899	U.P.U. size postcards allowed into G.B.
July 1900	Picture postcard magazine published.
Jan. 1902	Divided back postcards allowed in G.B.
21st June 1904	Metal Postcards not allowed in the post unless under cover.
5th Sept. 1905	Postcards posted in transparent envelopes no longer allowed in G.B.
June 1906	U.P.U. accepted the divided back postcard.
April 1907	Min. size of postcard raised to 4" by 2¾" from 3¼" by 2¼".
4th June 1907	Tinsel type postcards could only be sent under cover.
9th Sept 1911	First U.K. official aerial postcard.
4th Aug. 1914	First World War started.
14th Sept. 1915	Postcards to neutral countries subject to censorship.
2nd May 1916	Names etc. of H.M. Ships not allowed on postcards.
3rd June 1918	Postcard postage raised to 1d.
11th Nov. 1918	1st World War ended.
Dec. 1918	Censorship of postcards ended.

OTHER TITLES FROM PICTON PUBLISHING

SHIPS ON STAMPS *by E. W. Argyle* **£1.50* each**

For many years Mr E. W. Argyle has been one of the leading students of the depictions of ships on the postage stamps of the world. His many articles on the subject have been featured in marine publications in many countries and reflect great diligence and research work. Each part contains over 100 illustrations of both the stamps and their relevant original material, together with SG numbers, stamp denominations and countries of origin. **One**: The Royal Navy. **Two**: Passenger Liners. **Three**: Early Sailing Ships and Canoes. **Four**: Sailing Ships. **Five**: Local Craft. **Six**: Cross-Channel, River & Lake Passenger Ships. **Seven**: Cargo Ships, Oil Tankers. **Eight**: Sail & Paddle Auxiliary Vessels. **Nine**: Ships of the World's Navies. **Ten**: Miscellaneous Vessels, Index. **Eleven**: The Royal Navy (New Issues). **Twelve**: Passenger Liners of the World over 4,000 tons. **(N.B. Eleven & Twelve, £2 each)**

MUSIC ON STAMPS *in six parts by Sylvester Peat* **£1.50* each**

Sylvester Peat is the founder of the Philatelic Music Circle as well as being a noted musician, conductor and church organist. He has now turned his talent to writing and has produced a very fine series of works for the Thematic Collector. Each part contains over 150 illustrations of stamps and relevant biographical material of not only the well-known artists but also of the many minor geniuses who have been distinguished philatelically. **One**: A–B, Bach, Beethoven, Berlioz and Bartok. **Two**: C–F, Chopin, Debussy, Dvorak and Elgar. **Three**: G–L, Grieg, Handel, Haydn and Liszt. **Four**: M–R, Mahler, Mendlessohn, Mozart and Ravel. **Five**: S–Z, Schubert, Sibelius, Strauss and Tchaikovsky. **Six**: Musical Monarchs and National Anthems.

Now available, a new series

MORE MUSICIANS ON STAMPS **£2.00* each**

PICTON'S PHILATELIC HANDBOOK No. 1 **£4.00†**

A Provisional Guide to the Valuation of the Numeral Cancellations of England and Wales with notes on their use abroad, by M. A. Hewlett, BA. This is the first attempt to evaluate the 1844 and ordinary Duplex numeral postmarks. Many are scarce and worth up to £25 each according to Mr Hewlett's calculations. Essential to every dealer in postcards and GB Stamps. Collectors must buy it if they specialise in postmarks. Mr Hewlett compiles the postcard section of *Picton's Postcard Catalogue* in this new book he does for Postmark collectors what he did for postcard collectors - he has systematised the subject and evaluated the material for the first time.

RAILWAYS ON STAMPS *by A. M. Goodbody and C. A. Hart* **£1.50* each**

These four books are the first of a series which will reveal the many and varied locomotives, rolling stock, stations and trackside gear which appear on postage stamps of the world. These volumes deal with Eastern Europe, containing a wealth of illustration and technical detail. A 'must' for all railway enthusiasts and philatelists alike.

THE GREAT RAIDS *by Air Commodore J. H. Searby, DSO DFC*

A series of books on the raids by RAF Bomber Command during World War II. Each book in the series contains information and documents not before published, a complete list of the squadrons and crews who took part and is written superbly by an expert on the subject. He was there.

Part One: PEENEMUNDE. Soft Cover **£2.50†** Library Edition **£5†**

Part Two: ESSEN. THE BATTLE OF THE RUHR. Soft Cover **£3.50†** Library Edition **£5.50†**

AEROGRAMMES *by P. Jennings* **£4.50†**

1933 CENTENARY ISSUE OF THE FALKLAND ISLANDS *by R. N. Spafford* **£5†**

PRE-VICTORIAN STAMPS AND FRANKS *by Hewlett & Picton-Phillips* **£4†** *(new edition)*

GREAT BITTER LAKES POST *by Capt. B. Hill* **£6†**

THE WHALE'S TALE *by Frederick P. Schmitt* **£2.50†**

PRINTERS AND PRINTING IN PHILATELY *by John Alden* **£2.00†**

OFFICIAL RAILWAY POSTCARDS OF THE BRITISH ISLES **£4***

Postage and Packing ***=35p †=50p**

These titles available direct from PICTON PUBLISHING *or your local bookseller*

MEMBER OF THE POSTCARD TRADERS ASSOCIATION

ECCLESTON HOTEL

LONDON POSTCARD BOURSE

Our popular Postcard Bourse is held every month at The Eccleston Hotel, Eccleston Square, Victoria, London S.W.1 on the following Sundays in 1980

Jan 13	**May 11**	**Sept 14**
Feb 10	**June 8**	**Oct 12**
Mar 9	**July 13**	**Nov 9**
Apl 13	**Aug 10**	**Dec 14**

A JPA POSTCARD AUCTION WILL TAKE PLACE AFTER EACH FAIR

Admission Free 11 am — 5 pm

ALTRINCHAM
Cresta Court Hotel

Feb 17	**Aug 17**
Apl 20	**Oct 19**
June 15	**Dec 7**

BUY — SELL — EXCHANGE

We have one of the largest and most valuable stocks in the country and need to buy specialized and general collections. We cannot prove here that our buying prices are the best, but we can send you a copy of our current Buying List which gives examples of the prices paid. Before you sell, contact us. Although we are very pleased to purchase small collections both specialised and general, we particularly need collections in the £5,000 to £10,000 range or more.

RF Postcards

17 Hilary Crescent, Rayleigh, Essex Telephone: 0268 743222

DISCERNING COLLECTORS
from all over the world depend on
KEN LAWSON'S POSTCARD &
EPHEMERA AUCTION SALES
to improve or start collections
Held every fifth Monday at Caxton Hall, London, these 800-lot sales present the world of postcards at their most fascinating. General mixtures, etc at 2·30pm & more specialised items at 6pm. Viewing and retail tables (RF Postcards & Rosina Stevens) from 10am.
AUCTION DATES 1980
Mon Specialities
JAN 21 RAILWAY & TRAMWAY
FEB 25 SPORT & ENTERTAINMENT
MAR 31 MOTORING & AVIATION
APR 28 CHROMO & EARLY
JUNE 9 SETS & SILKS
Mon Specialities
JUL 14 COMIC & NOVELTY
SEPT 8 TUCK & FAULKNER
OCT 13 ADVERTISING & ART NOUVEAU
NOV 24 SHIPPING & MILITARY
DEC 22 CHILDREN & GLAMOUR
48-PAGE CATALOGUE WITH OVER 100 ILLUSTRATIONS SENT 2 WEEKS PRIOR
Year (10 sales) with prices realised £7·50 (GB inland) £9·50 (Europe) £15 (USA, Canada, Australia, NZ etc)
BIDDING BY POST OR IN PERSON • SAMPLE CATALOGUE 60p + 15p POST
MCC/SPA
MIDDLESEX COLLECTORS CENTRE SPECIALISED POSTCARD AUCTIONS
24 WATFORD RD WEMBLEY MIDDLESEX HA0 3EP
TEL: 01-908 2636
PTA MEMBER
The Jazzah
ZOO Series
PURE CONCENTRATED
Fry's Cocoa
ROYAL NAVAL EXHIBITION

"LIFE-BOAT
SATURDAY
VOTES FOR WOMEN WOW!!
WOOLLEN UNDERWEAR
AIGBURTH LORD ST.
The Diamond Jubilee
XMAS
FORCE
The Autocar
KILDAR
BETTER QUALITY CARDS
accepted
FOR SALE by AUCTION
by KEN LAWSON at Caxton Hall
Regular public auctions are held throughout the year usually at 5-weekly intervals. The Sale Total for 1978-9 season was £70,375. A 20% commission rate to sellers reduces by 5% when £50+ per lot is realised. Minimum value £8 lots please–no upper limit. Cash or cheque payment within ten days of sale.
Exceptional prices are now being obtained for top quality material in super condition
A FEW EXAMPLES ILLUSTRATED HERE FROM 1978/9 SALES
SEND FOR A SAMPLE CATALOGUE (75p)
and see if your collection of postcards matches up!
MCC/SPA
MIDDLESEX COLLECTORS CENTRE SPECIALISED POSTCARD AUCTIONS
24 WATFORD RD WEMBLEY MIDDLESEX HA0 3EP
TEL: 01-908 2636
PTA MEMBER

DAVID FIELD LIMITED

42, Berkeley Street, Mayfair, London W1X 5FP

WE STOCK THE FOLLOWING POSTCARD CATEGORIES

Actors
Actresses
Advertising
Aircraft
Airships
Angels
Animals
Art Repros
Artists
Babies
Beauties Photographic
Bicycles
Birds
Boxing
Bullfighting
Butterflies
Cars
Cats
Caves
Children
Churches
Comic
Christmas
Cricket
Disasters
Dogs
Early Cards
Easter
Erotica
Esperanto
Faith, Hope, Charity
Father Christmas
Film Stars
Firemen
Football
Give Aways
Heraldic
Horses
Large Letters
Lighthouses
Maps
Military
Moonlight
Music
Napoleon
Nelson
New Year
Novelty
Police
Political
Post Offices
Postal Themes
Publishers
Railways
Religion
Reward Cards
Romantic
Rough Seas
Royalty
Scouting
Ships
Silks
Sports and Games
Song Cards
Theatrical
Tuck Oilettes
W.W.1.
British/Foreign
Topographicals

Tel: 01-499 5252

WHY NOT GIVE US A TRY

INDEX

INDEX TO POSTMARKS